Here's to Nantucket

Here's to Nantucket

Recipes for the Good Life and Great Food

Jean-Charles Berruet
and
Jack Warner

Quinlan Press

Boston

a dmc book
Published by Quinlan Press, Inc.
131 Beverly Street
Boston, MA 02114

Project development: dmc associates, inc., Boston, MA
Design/management: Dennis Campbell
Photography: Cary Hazlegrove, Nantucket Filmworks,
  Nantucket, MA
Assistant to Chef Berruet: Lorna Dietz
Assistant to Mr. Warner: Beth Hanlon
Technical review: Joan Anderson
Composition: Xanadu Graphics, Cambridge, MA

ISBN: 0-933341-80-6

Library of Congress Card Number: 86-63437

Printed in the United States of America

First edition

To Earle and Jean MacAusland. Without them America would still be a faraway land.

Jean-Charles Berruet

And here's to Sam Roughton – for the good times.

Jack Warner

ACKNOWLEDGMENTS

Again, thanks to Beth Hanlon for her scrap
and hustle, to Lorna Dietz for her
enthusiasm, to Dennis Campbell for batting
cleanup, to Cary Hazlegrove for her winning
ways, and to Polly, who led us to a title.

CONTENTS

PREFACE

Nantucket seems to have more than its share of interesting people. I don't know if some deep thinking psychologist has ever concocted a fascination index, but if such a measuring device exists I recommend our little island as a place worthy of testing its maximum limits.

We cover the broad spectrum of human highs and lows. I suppose every small town does, but ours is a small town surrounded by water, so those who hit the lows have little chance to hide – but at least the rest of the world doesn't shine a light on them. Our high scorers also tend to be overlooked, and that's too bad. This book is about one of our real stars who could achieve that rarified atmosphere anywhere in the world but he has chosen Nantucket.

One cold winter day a few years ago a group of Nantucketers were sitting around my kitchen table having drinks and conversation. Occasionally the wind would rattle the windows on the northwest side of the house and I would toss another log into the woodstove. As the conversational ball bounced around the table, the wind picked up in velocity and began to make a series of high moaning cries that island folks know too well – especially if they live on the edge of the meadow on Upper Main Street. The room went still as we listened to the sound of the Nantucket winter. In the silence someone asked, "Where would you like to be right now? Anyplace in the world – where would you pick?"

As if on command we went around the table, each man naming places exotic or obscure or predictably sunny as the wind rammed the house. When the question came to the bearded, muscular man holding a goblet of red wine, he simply pointed a forefinger downward. And in a distinct French accent Jean-Charles Berruet said, "This is where I want to be and it's where I always want to be – right here, Nantucket."

I looked across the table at my friend and thought, here is a truly content human being – one of the favored few who knows who he is and what he wants from life.

This is his story. I hope you'll enjoy reading of the feast he has made of life and I hope my pen has caught the essence of this special person.

Jack Warner

Here's to Nantucket

Why Nantucket?

One evening a very distinguished couple visited me in the kitchen of my restaurant, the Chanticleer. It was Monsieur and Madame Patrice Pages. He is the heir to a noble French family whose family seat and vineyard is the Chateau Fourcas Hosten. They were kind enough to come into the kitchen and praise the meal they had just concluded. We chatted briefly and I learned that this handsome pair was on their honeymoon. They said they intended to return to the Chanticleer the next day for lunch before they went to the airport to resume their honeymoon travels. As they turned to leave, Madame Pages said something quietly to her husband. He smiled with a hint of embarrassment and said, "Yes, my wife is right. We must ask you, why Nantucket? With all the great cities in America to tempt a French chef, how did you ever find this little jewel of land in the middle of the ocean?"

I responded with a chuckle and said that someday if I had enough time and enough wine I would tell that story.

Now it seems that I have been lucky enough to reach that moment.

The French are a people who pride themselves on logic. I think it is most logical to tell my story by beginning at the beginning.

I was born in Brittany to a humble family in the city of Nantes which lies at the mouth of the Loire river. Muscadet is the wine of Brittany, and my birthplace is in the heart of Muscadet country. One of my sharpest memories is of my grandfather's small vineyard. It was not a commercial venture – just wine for the family table that we would drink with the fresh seafood that comes in abundance from that rough Breton Sea, which is known to the rest of the world as the Bay of Biscay. I remember picking the grapes of that vineyard every year. We'd make the wine and then even in my earliest days I'd drink that wine with my grandfather, my mother's father. The wine was not put into liters, but rather into small bottles like a half bottle. The reasoning behind the use of these bottles was some more French logic. It's easier to drink a small bottle than a big bottle and in this Muscadet country they drink a bit. They call those bottles *fillettes*, which means small girl. They pop open one of those little girls at maybe nine o'clock in the morning and have a glass of white wine – they do that from time to time through the day.

It's poor country down there. At that time, with the country occupied by the Germans, it was even poorer. My family wasn't wealthy. After France fell to the Germans my father worked in a chemical plant as an engineer. The food we ate with that Muscadet was very simple. On the little bit of land we had we raised chickens and rabbits and grew all kinds of vegetables. It took lots of hard work to coax every bit of food we could out of that plot of earth. The cooking was done with the extensive use of garlic – but at least we were eating. Many people in Europe were not.

Helping my grandfather make wine, drinking a glass of that wine at the table with a fish that I caught in the Loire, those are the good memories. There aren't too many because the war was all around us. Those memories are the bad part of the past.

I was just a little kid when the world was going through all that savagery. It seemed to me then that it was just the way life was. I was small enough to crawl under the trains and steal potatoes that had fallen to the ground. So small that the German sentries wouldn't see me. It was like a game. I knew it was dangerous but at that age, it was our sport.

The Germans had built great concrete bunkers under the water in the harbor in Nantes. These were pens for the U-boats. The allies bombed them and the approaches to them over and over. In my memory, it seems they bombed the first bridge across the river every day.

I remember fleeing Nantes in the night – my mother, my older sister, and me. The city was on fire from the bombs. The allies bombed the city from high altitudes and the bombs fell erratically. There were flames everywhere. It was as though the whole world was on fire. I remember seeing a man pushing a hand cart with a pile of bodies on it. Over five thousand people were killed in the city that night.

My father was not with us then because the Germans had put him in a concentration camp.

It was in 1943 when the Gestapo came into our house. I remember that. I can't tell you what day it was but everything else I remember very clearly. It was nighttime. That's when the Gestapo were the busiest – in the night – like rats. There were three of them. They came right into the house and sat down at the dining room table. One of them took out a gun – a luger pistol – and put it on the table. They were nice to us. They were these three pleasant guys who started chatting to these two little kids – my sister and me. So we started talking to them. My mother had gone into the little alcove right off the dining room where there was a small gas range that she did our cooking on. This was the kitchen. She rushed into the dining room and slapped us both – very hard. Wham! Right across the face. She told us not to speak to these men. That was the beginning of that night.

The Gestapo found guns buried in our garden. They found some papers. My father, you see, was a member of the underground and he moved British fliers through our house to the coast so they could return to England. There were names and dates for pickups of arms drops. The Gestapo knew these things. My father was in an operation called

Buckmaster which after the war became well-known in England and France for the bravery of the people involved. Someone had turned my father in.

When the Gestapo came into the house, my mother had picked up dishes and other things off a sideboard and gone into the little kitchen. She filled a big pot with water and said she was going to heat the water to wash the dishes. What she actually did, right there under the nose of the Gestapo, was to take all of my father's papers that she could grab and put them on the fire under the pot. These papers contained very involved information about the Buckmaster group – maps marked with dates and places for arms drops, places to find or hide allied pilots, places and people who would hide allied pilots, places where arms were buried. While the Gestapo sat there, my mother burned that information. They never smelled it. She burned the entire pile of information with them sitting so close to the fire. Years later she told us she was terribly frightened, but she certainly didn't act like it then. She had every right to be. I think maybe they would have killed her on the spot. So that information they never got. Sometimes they weren't as smart as they thought.

When my father came home that night the Gestapo arrested him and took him away. He spent the rest of the war in a concentration camp. He was very badly treated and his health never recovered from it. I believe my father's death was caused by the way he was treated in the concentration camp.

When we fled from Nantes we moved to the village where my grandfather lived, a place much smaller than Nantucket called Le Pouliguen. It was right on the coast – a fishing place. Mostly sardines, good firm fresh sardines. We ate them often and with pleasure. The world was in turmoil but there was the fish and the Muscadet and I was a little boy and I could catch fish. I loved to do that then as I do now.

I remember in that village when the bombers would come we would drag the mattress under a table and we would all hide under the table. I think of that now and chuckle. How we thought we were safe – hiding under the table from the bombs.

When the war finally ended we moved back to Nantes.

It seems as though I have always been interested in food. Preparation, cooking – it had my attention even when I was a little fellow. I think it might have been because of my father. I admired him very much and he loved to cook. He'd cook the meal every Sunday. That's the big meal of the week in France and I think that even now in most families it is the man's job to cook the Sunday meal. They love it. I think many men – perhaps Frenchmen in particular – are frustrated chefs. Of course this is because the man is not stuck with cooking everyday as the wife often is. The woman knows she has to cook and she might resent it. My mother hates cooking and I know many women who feel that same way – there might even be one living at my house. It's a pain in the ass to them because they have to do it. Strange, but it is most often the guy who really likes cooking. He has the pan, the special knife, the special whisk and once a week he uses these tools and his skills and really enjoys it because he doesn't have to do this as work and, therefore, it isn't a chore, it's pleasure.

Every Sunday my father's cooking was an adventure. The meal was more a long lunch than a dinner. All the kids would help, but I would be very involved and it was a joy. It still is.

My growing up was quite different from American boys. The pleasures of my youth were fishing and baking cakes. Even when I was very small I would ask my mother for flour and water and I'd make a cake. By the time I was twelve I had a sense of what I wanted to do with my life. My father had been an officer in the French Navy. He had gone to the Naval Cadet School. From the beginning, however, in my earliest thoughts I knew I had no intention of going there.

One day at school they gave us tests that were meant to determine the work we were best suited for and they talked with us about what we would like to work at. They had this conversation with no parents sitting, staring, so you could speak what was in your heart. I told them I didn't want to go to the Naval Cadet School. "I want to cook," I said, "I want to be a chef."

They called my parents in for a conference and they told them that I didn't want to be a Naval officer, I wanted to cook. My father was a little disappointed, but I don't think too much so because he had his own feel for cooking and he loved to go to restaurants. Oh! How he loved to go to restaurants to try new dishes and different wines. For meals he cooked at home he had his own wine – marvelous wine that he would choose very carefully and that I would occasionally steal from him just as carefully.

A friend of mine, Michel LeBorgne, was an apprentice cook with me in France. He is now the executive chef of The New England Culinary Institute in Montpelier, Vermont. We were speaking recently and he reminded me of a day we were running a race together against other teams of boys and I said that if we won I would steal a bottle of my father's wine and we would drink it together. Michel reminded me that we won the race and I came up with the wine. He said he still remembers drinking that wonderful bottle of wine. It was so good we both remembered what it was. Clos Vougeot, a burgundy – a wine so marvelous the memory has lasted over thirty years. Now I think to myself, My God, how could I have done such a thing.

By the way, Michel's school in Vermont is tops. It is an outstanding place to learn the skills of cooking. It is a small school with about sixty students. They have their own restaurant and bakery right there in Montpelier. If cooking is what you or one of your kids want, that is the place. I recommend it highly.

In France in those days there were no culinary institutes to teach you the profession of cooking. There was only the ages old system of apprenticeship. For a youngster the key was to find a place to apprentice. I was a very lucky young man finding my special situation, which came about through the travail that my father had experienced in the concentration camp.

When I was about thirteen years old we moved to Tours. This is the center of the Loire region. It is the crib of the French language. The purest French is spoken there. In Tours there was a priest who had been in prison with my father. Also in Tours was a man called Charles Barrier who had a restaurant appropriately called, Restaurant Charles Barrier, which was designated as a three star restaurant by Michelin – one of the seventeen three stars in all of France. This would be one of the outstanding places in France – in the entire world – to learn cooking. This priest and Charles Barrier were friends and because I was my father's son I was taken ahead of a long waiting list to become an apprentice to this brilliant, demanding, difficult genius of the world of food.

From the 1940's through the 1970's Charles Barrier would be on any list of the ten greatest chefs in France. Because of the French devotion to great food and those who cook it, Barrier was a famous man. I believe this fame meant absolutely nothing to him. He cared about two things only – food preparation on the highest level and service of the finest order in his restaurant. Barrier was a tall, balding, thick chested man of perhaps two hundred and fifty pounds who many people might have thought was phlegmatic until they saw him in temper, which was on the order of a volcano erupting. When he felt the need, he would reach out and wallop you and then return at once to the business at hand.

Charles Barrier became a major figure in my early professional life, and in many ways he remains one. It is in the nature of the apprentice system in France that the mentor assumes the role of the parent. He has complete control of the apprentice. The process begins in a very formal manner which emphasizes the seriousness of the undertaking. The apprentice program in France is under the control and direction of the Department of Commerce of the National Government. A contract is signed between the parents, the Chamber of Commerce, the Mayor of the town and the mentor. It is a very solemn, very serious business. The apprentice stands silently, probably numbly, and watches the signing of this contract which he understands transfers him totally into the hands of this new person.

My first brief conversation with the great chef led me to believe that my new parent was one very tough guy. The next three years proved me to be one hundred percent correct.

As you might imagine, the apprentice begins at the very bottom. He does the basics. He cleans the kitchen – cleaning meaning to make spotless. He peels the potatoes. He cleans and scrapes and cuts vegetables. The most menial jobs are reserved for the apprentice.

In the morning you rise at five o'clock, you get on a bus or your bicycle and go to the market. The chef is already there. He appraises, he talks, he makes the bargain and picks the fish and the fowl and vegetables for the day. You watch him as he makes his purchases. You watch him all the time. When he jerks a thumb at a crate, you pick it up and carry it to the truck. It is an intense beginning to the day. You learn a lot about arguing with people.

Back at the restaurant you work until just before one o'clock. Then you hand the chef the little book that you must carry with you. He marks the correct time in the book because you are now leaving for school. When you arrive at school the time is noted again. The same procedure occurs later in the afternoon when you leave school and return to the restaurant. It is very strict. There is no fooling around. There better be no gaps of time.

It is not completely accurate, however, to say there is no fooling around because since we were just kids, of course there was some fooling around. My memories of some of those escapades make me smile even now.

We lived on the premises above the restaurant – six of us – all apprentices living there. There was a wall around the courtyard in back. We'd climb over the wall and sneak into town. Our pay amounted to about five bucks a month. So, as you can imagine, we couldn't do very much, but we were still always frantic to get out and walk around the town at night. The chef got a dog to keep us from climbing over the wall and his wife watched us like a hawk. Between the wife watching and the dog snarling, it was quite a stunt to sneak out. If you were successful it usually wasn't a real triumph because you knew that when you tried to sneak back in you'd end up getting a kick in the ass from the boss.

One memorable kick that I got was on a day that I decided to do a little fishing in the restaurant. In the downstairs area was a big tank with live trout and pickerel and crayfish. It was bigger than the one that I have now at the Chanticleer. I got myself a piece of string and used a safety pin as a hook early one morning and was busy trying to catch myself a trout when the chef walked in and caught me. Holy smoke! That was a tough day. I tell you it was tough.

All the restaurant's ham and pork were made from Barrier's own pigs that we raised. The chef always watched these animals carefully. One day when all the apprentices were really angry at him we let the pigs loose out onto the street. This was a busy street in Tours. The sight of the pigs running wild and the chef waving his arms after them was a great treat for us apprentices. We giggled and laughed about it just like I am now.

We did so many things to lighten the long hours, to have some laughs, to just be kids.

One day Charles Barrier bought a new car. France was just getting over the war. It was 1956. The first new Citroen was produced. The boss had gone to Paris to pick up the new car and when he brought the car into the city it was a major event. The first and only one in Tours. The chef and Madame and all the neighborhood marched around the new car admiring it. It was a beauty – elegant, shiny black, with high rounded front fenders and big silver headlights. It was clearly his pride and joy.

The next morning the chef had to go to a meeting. He took his old truck – the car, of course, was too valuable to use. So, the new car is sitting there. We all jumped in – the six apprentices. I'm behind the wheel. None of us know how to drive. It was the first automatic we'd seen. We fiddled with things in the front, turned on the motor, next thing we know, the car is in gear and we bang into a truck parked in front. Oh my God! I thought my heart would stop. We were all terrified. We leapt out of the car and raced off in all directions – afraid to speak, afraid to look at one another. That was my closest call. I tell you, you wouldn't believe how angry he was. He almost kicked me out. I guess the friendship between my father and the priest in the camp probably saved me.

There were lessons that you learned the hard way that stay with you. There were three or four chickens lined up on the fire. I was supposed to watch them. However, I didn't pay very good attention – they got burned. The chef came over and looked at them. He looked at me.

He said, "The chickens are ruined. Leave them on the fire now."

When they were well burned, he had me take the chickens off. That's all I got to eat for the next four or five days – burnt chicken. I never burned another one.

One day we had pickerel that we were to dip in boiling water for a minute to blanch, then pull it out and take off the scales. Just in and out and scale it. I left it in too long and ruined it. He took it off my pay. He charged me twenty francs so I had no money for a month.

Charles Barrier was meticulous. Everything had to be done just right. He started with the basics and built from that. He was devoted to the classic cuisine. He did not change things. He developed each dish to the highest art he could achieve. He never experimented with his recipes once they reached what he felt was the ultimate level achievable.

As an apprentice, I quickly learned that the juices made and saved from the cooking of meat or fish or vegetables are critical in the refining of a dish. This liquid is so important that in France it is called *fonds,* which means the basics and that is just what it is – basic. In America this juice is called stock and it is the foundation of soups, gravies, aspics and of course the sauces that are critical to classic French food.

Whether you want to be elegant or simple in your cooking – as long as you want to be at the stove at all – you should master the skill of making stock. It is no big deal. Every apprentice soon learns it.

Early in the morning the Chef would announce to an apprentice that today he was making – let's say, chicken stock. All parts of the chicken that are ignored in a recipe would be handed to the young man. Necks, feet, legs, wings. A large pot, for a restaurant probably forty gallons, is filled with cold water. I recommend you use your biggest pot at home too because you can freeze the stock when you are through. It is imperative that the water is cold. Experience taught the great chefs that hot water seals the flavor into the food. What we want to achieve is to get the flavor into the liquid when we bring the cold water to a boil. So, let us say our pot of what you would call chicken scraps is boiling now. Ah, you see now all sorts of detritus comes to the top – blood, bits and pieces of skin and that all forms a scum at the top. You see, you learn in cooking as in life that it isn't necessarily the best that gets to the top.

You skim off the scum. Then you put vegetables in. Basic vegetables and remember, celery is a basic – maybe the basic. Then of course, carrots and onions, root vegetables and always a *bouquet garni* – a bundle of herbs.

The pot keeps boiling and more and more things – we'll call them things – come to the top. We keep skimming that off. When the top of the liquid is reasonably clear, the heat is turned down. The liquid cooks slowly for three or four hours. Then you strain everything. Squeeze your cheesecloth and extract every bit of rich, flavored liquid from the chicken parts and vegetables. Throw away the bones and vegetables. Put the liquid back on the fire and simmer longer if you wish. The more you reduce the liquid the stronger the stock flavor.

Now, since we are doing chicken we take it from the fire and place it in the refrigerator. The fat from the chicken will congeal on the top. Let it sit until it is well congealed then remove this fat. Simmer a bit more if you wish.

All stocks are done in this method with the exception of refrigerating to help eliminate the fat of the chicken. This process is the way we apprentices were taught to make the bases of what I now call stock.

Naturally, I've included the recipes for *fonds* that were taught me by Charles Barrier. I learned the basics from the best.

As my days at the Restaurant Charles Barrier accumulated, so did my proficiency in the kitchen. Every apprentice strives to prepare himself to pass the examination that is given to achieve the Certificate of Professional Aptitude. This exam is not to be taken until the apprentice has a minimum of three years experience. Without the certificate one cannot own or put his name on a restaurant in France. France feels that this regulation protects the food industry of which the nation is justifiably proud. Anyone can finance a restaurant but the place cannot be operated in the name of the financier, it must be designated to someone with a certificate. This is one reason the apprenticeship years are so endlessly demanding. A chef is jealous of his position and his honor in the profession. Charles Barrier certainly was. He would remark that we would carry his name as having been his pupils. I know that it was important to him that we achieved skills as close to perfection as he could drive us. The many successes of his apprentices demonstrate what a good coach he was. He was great – the toughest guy I have ever met in my life. The service in his restaurant was probably the finest in France. When Georges Pompidou was President of France he flew to Tours every Sunday possible to lunch at Restaurant Charles Barrier. Mon Dieu! What a testimonial! What a reputation! Each apprentice was made to understand that Charles Barrier's name was on every dish that left that kitchen. Sometimes he reminded us the hard way with a kick in the ass or a bang on the head. Sometimes that is the way it has to be.

Strange how our view changes when we get older. I usually go to France every year to select some of the wines for the Chanticleer's next season, and sometimes I bring a few of my people from the restaurant. We always visit Charles Barrier. He treats us like kings. Now he is such a warm, nice guy, yet I know what a tough son of a bitch he is. I have great respect for him. I think of him as a great big guy. Now when I see him he seems small, then he was like a giant. He formed a lot of apprentices into successful chefs. Like my friend K.C. Jones, Charles Barrier is a great coach.

Those three years are the hardest years of your life in my profession. If you last long enough to get your certificate, you are set. I would guess that there is a sixty percent casualty rate for apprentices.

The examination consists of written questions which are given a certain weight in the marking, but the most important segment of the testing occurs when the applicant is directed to take one piece of paper from each of three stacks. Each paper directs that the applicant prepare (1) a particular appetizer, (2) a main course, (3) a dessert. The dishes are prepared and cooked under the scrutiny of accomplished chefs and teachers of gastronomy. Of course, the moment of truth arrives when they taste each dish.

I was successful on my first attempt at certification. I remained with my mentor awhile longer. However, I was distracted by the events of the world around me. France was engaged in a war in Algeria. It was a guerrilla war between people who were civilians one moment, killers the next. Despite the generations of French settlement, our troops were seen as colonial oppressors. The Algerian War brutalized everyone it touched.

My National Service time was facing me. I had a major decision to make as to how I would serve. I resolved this by becoming a paratrooper. I served in the Army for just over two years. Some of that time was spent in combat in Algeria. Among the books I have in my house is a photographic essay about the Algerian War entitled, *Les Dieux Meurent En Algerie – The Gods Died in Algeria.* The title is very appropriate. Many of the gods of France died in Algeria.

I returned from Algeria to the greatest city in the world – Paris. Paris is the one place in the world that can wipe away the grime and stench and perhaps the memories of war. I returned from Algeria to that city of beauty and went to work at once in a little hide-away restaurant just outside the city. This was a great, great place run by the fellow who owned Maxim's, but it shall be nameless – the work, the people, the place.

It was all beautiful and it attracted the beautiful people. High Society, movie stars, powerful businessmen, politicians. They all came and they brought their girlfriends and their mistresses – seldom, if ever, their wives. Why to this particular place? Who knows? But they came. The place had six small rooms. There were two chambermaids who were our good friends. They would leave the curtains in the rooms up at night. You wouldn't believe the things we saw. Everything imaginable! We had to go outside to see into those rooms. There was much rushing outside from the kitchen to look in windows in astonishment and delighted, stifled laughter. The chef would go nuts yelling at us to remain at our posts. Then when the news of events of one of the rooms was simply too juicy, he would throw up his hands and race outside to have a peek. What else could he do? What a place! What laughs we had!

Then the time came for me to travel to England. It had been in my mind for some time. I had no trouble finding reasons for crossing the Channel. I wanted to learn English and I knew that all the great classic French chefs went to England. Escoffier worked most of his life at the Savoy in London. And education aside, there was the fact that the pay was better in England.

I knew that French chefs are a valuable commodity everywhere in the world and it was my intention to see lots of the world.

In England in the 1960's the big hotels still had brigades of help in their kitchens. My first job was at the Queen's Hotel in Manchester which was owned by the Ind Coope Brewery. There were more than forty of us – probably fifty – preparing each meal. My job was *Chef de Partie,* which means that I was responsible for one particular item on the menu. The Chef de Partie has what is called a station. My station was the fish dishes. There are stations for meat, chicken, vegetables, dessert and any specialty the chef designates.

After a year at the Queen's, I moved to another large hotel in the Ind Coope chain, the Leofric in the city of Coventry. I still didn't speak English. At least the people I tried to talk with didn't seem to think I spoke English. My efforts to learn the language had not been as successful as I wished.

To my great good fortune I found a teacher one night in a little pub in Coventry. She was a slim beauty from the lowlands of Scotland who was working in the city as a secretary.

After some months of work at the Leofric and continuing study in my English lessons, the Scots girl and I decided to embark on an adventure. We would go to Wales and work there together.

We Bretons believe that Brittany is a much more special place than the rest of France. The Welsh are just as sure that they are of a special culture, far above the British – and we all know how the Irish feel about themselves and the world. There is a reason for this. It runs in our blood. The fact is that we Bretons, Welsh and Irish are all Celts. In the case of the Welsh and the Bretons there are some amazing proofs. A Welshman can converse a bit with a native Breton, some of the words being identical to the ear. When a Breton first stands and listens to the Welsh National Anthem played at the start of one of their beloved international rugby matches, his eyes will probably blink as he realizes he is listening to the same melody as the Breton National song.

The Welsh have resisted the English and their ways since the beginning of time. They work unceasingly to protect their culture. They are a wonderful people.

Perhaps it was natural for a Scots girl and a Breton boy to go to Wales. It seemed like it would be the right place for us and it was.

I had no problem finding a position there. I think one of the few things in life that young people can count on is this: if you have a good knowledge of food preparation, work diligently at using this knowledge and earn good references, one can find work anywhere in the world.

Our situation in Wales was a memorable one in an idyllic country setting. It was my first employment as head chef. The place was called the Bontddu Hall Hotel. It served a town called Dolgelly and a county named Merionethshire. I don't think things can be much more Welsh than that.

The hotel was actually a wonderful Victorian pile of stone with ramparts and battlements set on the crest of a hill overlooking Cardigan Bay. A brook tumbled past the front door down into the sea. When lunch was finished I'd take my fishing rod and walk the stream as it twisted through that wild, beautiful country. Many afternoons I'd catch as many as twenty trout. I would keep a few of the fish and feature them as a special at dinner that evening.

One of the greatest advantages of my profession is that it is possible to work in a place where you also want to live. Wales taught me that. It was a great place and a wonderful time. I was near the ocean and the trout streams and more importantly I was near the woman I love. The Scots girl gave up her secretarial work and learned the business of waiting on tables at the Bontddu Hall Hotel. We made such a good team that I thought we should be together always, so Anne Todd of Peebles, Scotland became Mrs. Jean-Charles Berruet and I think we still make a hell of a good team.

After we were married we decided to go to France. My English was improving and it seemed a good idea for my wife to be at ease with the French language. We went to a restaurant near the town of Chablis. We worked a season there. I ran the kitchen and Anne worked the front of the house. It went very well. So did my wife's French. She quickly became fluent. I was impressed – I still am.

We left Burgundy for a job in northeastern France in a city on the Meuse River. It was better pay that brought us to what must be the most melancholy place in the so-called civilized world. A nasty place. A place of tears. A place of death. A place called Verdun.

Verdun is a small city of perhaps 25,000, but its name is written very large in the history of France. Even before Caesar came to France, Verdun was an important strategic military outpost. Throughout the centuries control of the fortress of Verdun has been contested by the armies of France and the Boche, but it was in the First World War that Verdun became a word the uttering of which brings silence and the glistening of tears to any group of French people.

From February to November in the year 1916 the German effort to smash the French line at Verdun caused the death in battle of over seven hundred and fifty thousand men. A generation of young French men was wiped out in ten months of unrelenting carnage. When Anne and I arrived at Verdun, we quickly learned that there was no place in the ground around Verdun where a shovel or a plow could turn the earth without revealing a shell fragment, the brass handle of a bayonet, a piece of rotting uniform, and all too often the remains of a soldier.

Picking mushrooms in the spring is something I have always enjoyed. It should be a happy-go-lucky experience. In the woods around Verdun, however, it was a thoughtful, sobering business because it was impossible to ignore the constant reminders of the mementoes of destruction that protruded from the fresh green earth.

Ironically, that terrible place has many happy memories for Anne and me – our son Marc was born there and it was in Verdun that our American adventure and our Nantucket life were initiated.

Verdun was completely destroyed in both World Wars and was rebuilt again after the Second War. I worked in a fine new hotel called The Bellevue that was built to accommodate the many tourists who visit the forts and cemeteries. An American military base was located near the town and I began cooking at private parties for the Americans. These were the first Americans I had met. I liked them and their open, friendly ways.

After a couple of years in Verdun I was ready to run my own place. I was sure that my knowledge of cooking and restaurant management was sufficient. There was one problem – one that most of us have encountered at some stage of our lives. We had no money. However, I had heard of a program in which the French government would make a loan to a qualified chef to enable him to begin a new business.

I looked and looked for a restaurant. I would investigate any possibility. Finally I found one in Lyon. I brought Anne to see it. The place had been closed down for a year. It was a decrepit, spooky kind of place, but I was certain that we could make it work. The price was quite reasonable. On the train back we decided to try it. I would go to the government association and ask for the credit necessary. I was confident we could pay it back.

Well, I went through all the paper work with the association, showed my certificate and letters of recommendation and they said O.K., now we will go to the bank.

So the banker said, "Fine, now who will cosign this note with you?"

I told them, "I don't have any money, my family doesn't have any money. I don't know anyone who could cosign for me, that's why I'm here."

They said, "That's too bad. We can't help you."

Foolishness. The whole thing – the government program that helps you only if you don't need their help.

By this time my English was understandable and Anne and I had made some good friends at the military base. I was offered the job as chef in the officers' mess. The pay was very good and there was access to the finest ingredients available. It was a great place to work, but I knew it was just a stop on a journey to someplace else. Although where that someplace else was, I couldn't have guessed.

One of our good friends on the base was James Durnin. He is Marc's godfather. He and his wife live out in Arizona now. He had helped make the job at the mess available. He had a friend, a Major Baron, who asked one day why we didn't go to the States. "A chef like you would do well there," he said, "and I know a guy who has a food magazine in America. Maybe he would help you get located."

Just like that. I think it's very American to offer a hand like that. It's one of the things that makes this such a great country.

So, I wrote to this man at a New York address that the fellow gave me. His name was Earle MacAusland. He was the owner and publisher of *Gourmet Magazine.* In my letter I asked how a French chef with good references went about getting a job in America. It was a simple letter, but it would change our lives.

I received a quick answer from Mr. MacAusland. He said he could help me get a job in a restaurant but that his own chef, René, was retiring and returning to France and he asked if I would be interested in the position. I returned an affirmative answer and was instructed to go to *Gourmet*'s Paris office for further conversation.

In the Paris office of *Gourmet* I was thoroughly quizzed and checked out. Soon after that I was told that Mr. MacAusland would like to hire me but that I must be willing to sign a three year contract. That was O.K. with me. I figured we'd spend that time in America, save some money, see the country and then come back to France and open a restaurant.

There were a couple of matters I had to resolve before I would sign the contract. I said that my wife would not work; she should not be considered part of the deal. She had the baby to care for and that was enough work. Then there was the question of airplane tickets. I wouldn't admit it but we did not have enough money to fly to America or much of anyplace else. That was quickly agreed on also. So everything was settled. We would go to America.

I was told by the people in *Gourmet*'s Paris office that a house would be found for us in Nantucket which was where Mr. MacAusland kept a summer home. That was the first time I heard the word Nantucket. I went back to the base and asked all the guys if they knew where Nantucket was. No one had any idea. We got out an Atlas. Anne and I and a bunch of guys crowded around the table. Finally we found it – a pinpoint on the map.

Anne was appalled. "Oh my God," she said, "it's a speck in the middle of the ocean."

I said, "Don't worry about it," but I thought, "Oh, wow."

We gave what things we could to the family and sold some stuff while we waited for our visas to come through. That didn't take long. I learned later that that was because Mr. MacAusland was a close friend of Senator Barry Goldwater.

So, we headed for America. We boarded the 707 Air France plane on 15 September, 1966 – the three of us, Anne and I and our ten month old baby boy. We had three suitcases and five hundred dollars. In one of the suitcases I had my tools, my knives and whisks. Our destination was New York. We were excited about seeing the great city. I think every foreigner who comes to America has an almost fearful delight at the thought of visiting the most famous city in America, the place of huge buildings, jammed streets, jostling crowds and tough guys carrying revolvers.

There was, however, a small problem nagging at the corner of my mind. How are we going to find this guy MacAusland?

I needn't have worried. No sooner were we off the plane than a handsome, slender, grey haired man with cool blue eyes approached us. He was wearing a pin-striped suit and appeared to be a proper gentleman. He introduced himself as Earle MacAusland. What he appeared to be, he was, then and always – a gentleman in every way.

Mr. MacAusland informed us that he had booked a room for us at a hotel right there by the airport. O.K., here we are in America and we get in a big limo and go to this hotel, have a snack and go to sleep. New York City was right out there somewhere. The next morning the chauffeur called the room, we went down and got into the limo and we drove for almost an hour. We didn't see any skyscrapers and then we were at another airport called LaGuardia. Mr. MacAusland was there standing beside a twin engine airplane which we soon realized was his. He introduced us to his pilot, Tony Benjamin. As our suitcases were stowed, Mr. MacAusland told us we were heading for Nantucket. We were quickly airborne. It was a cloudy day. We never saw a skyscraper – not one. That was it for New York City. I watched Anne and I knew she was uncomfortable in the small plane with a baby in her lap and nothing to see outside but clouds.

Mr. MacAusland chatted with us a bit during the flight and was astonished to discover that my wife was from Scotland. He made us know at once that he was very proud of his Scottish heritage. That was one of the many things about him that I always admired.

Finally, the plane came out of the clouds and I looked down and saw this fishhook shaped piece of land lying in the sea. I could see two smaller islands strung out to the east of the big fishhook.

"That's Nantucket," Mr. MacAusland said. "The two smaller islands are Tuckernuck and Muskeget."

I could feel Anne's eyes on me, so I kept staring down so she couldn't see my face. I was thinking, "My God, we've made a deal to live on an American Indian Reservation and everyone in Europe knows how bad the Americans treat the Indians."

Things became more of a puzzle when we landed. An attractive, pleasant lady walked out to greet us but she was wearing blue jeans and some kind of casual shoes that looked like slippers. This lady is Mrs. Jean MacAusland. She leads us over to – I can't believe it! – an old wooden body station wagon. I thought, What the hell is going on? This lady is not dressed like I figured a rich American lady would and the car is a piece of junk.

Now I know the lady is as stylish and unpretentious as anyone can be and the car – the 1937 Packard Station Wagon – I think is a thing of beauty. But then!!

Things did not get better that first morning. In fact the biggest jolt was just ahead. Right up the road, you might say. We piled into the Packard with Mrs. MacAusland at the wheel. After a brief time on a badly paved road, we headed off across the moors on a dirt road. And we stayed on dirt roads – once or twice crossing a paved road, but from what I could see the island roads were not paved. That seemed appropriate because to my horror and Anne's – and she says she'll never forget how shocked she was – the houses that we saw were wood! All of them, all wood. Only the poorest of the poor in Europe lived in wooden houses. They were shacks for those who couldn't afford a real house of stone and mortar. What kind of a place was this Nantucket? Dirt roads and wooden houses?

In the minutes before we reached our destination my concern and, I guess you could say, confusion, were very intense. We traveled along a narrow, bumpy and rutted, sandy roadway that twisted through heavy growth of wild grapes, short, windblown pines and tangled red berry bushes. My God! There was no room for any car to pass from the other direction. I thought we must be going to a log cabin in the woods. The car nosed down into a little ravine past what I recognized as apple and pear trees. The road widened and before us on a rise was a long, low single story house. Wooden naturally. We got out of the car very slowly because Anne and I were in a state of shock. There was a garage on the right. I looked over there and saw two Rolls Royces. I turned back and there was a uniformed butler standing to help us with the luggage we didn't have.

Inside the house was like every European's idea of Hollywood. Elegant bedrooms and bathrooms. The kitchen was perfect – it had everything any chef would ever need. The dining room was a great long beamed, low ceiling room with an exquisite twenty foot marble table. But most importantly, on this side of the house, right out my kitchen window, was the ocean – a part that I soon learned was called Polpis Harbor. I saw an old wooden cabin cruiser moored out there. It looked liked a water going version of the station wagon. I wasn't surprised when Mr. MacAusland told me it was his, as was the Boston Whaler anchored closer to shore. He said he'd had the cabin cruiser built in Hawaii. It was called the *Malahini.* In the distance, beyond the boats I could see the white sandy beach of a low lying piece of land.

"So," I say to myself, "Maybe this guy likes fishing. Maybe this job's not going to be so bad after all. And here's the ocean right here beside us. That's never bad. So let's see how this all turns out."

I hear some people say that one particular piece of luck changed their life. I believe it. In my case, two things joined in one place to form an event of great good fortune.

First, there was America and to top it – Nantucket. Of all the great places in this great country, Anne and I found the best. I am an American citizen now and proud of it. It is my country. Nantucket is my place. Yet, I will never lose my pride and attachment to my native Brittany. If some night you watch me listen to a recording of the wonderful, stirring sound of our native Breton bagpipes, I do not deny that you might see moisture glistening in my eyes. That music moves in my Breton blood but now it is an American heart that pumps that blood.

Coming to America and Nantucket was not in itself the crown of our good luck. That came from the fate that put us in the hands of the MacAuslands and brought me the opportunity to work for, to serve, and be befriended by Earle MacAusland who was truly a prince among men.

I would say I was almost instantly happy on the island. The surroundings were perfect for my likes. For me there has to be water. I was born in November and I am told that's related to a water sign. There has to be space – country space. I'm not a city man. I've worked in Paris, in London, in Coventry and in Palm Beach. Those kinds of places are not for me. I need the quiet of the land, but I couldn't live in the Midwest. I'm captivated by mountains – for awhile – but the fields and the mountains stay the same to me. The ocean changes all the time. It's full of emotion for me – strength, love, sometimes maybe fear. Water is always alive.

Brittany is also a place of water and space. Claude Monet once referred to Brittany as a place of "savage beauty." I think his description explains the difference between the place of my youth and my Nantucket Island home. The coast of Brittany is a hard rocky shoulder of granite that exists in a tormented relationship with a furious sea. The beaches are a stoney edge of land that collide abruptly with the water. Far out from the beach, sharp, ragged pinnacles of rocks seem to jut up in the spray they create. Nature is very dramatic in Brittany. The storms are frequent, sudden, angry explosions. The distant reaches of Brittany are known as *Finis-terre* – the end of the earth. It seems an appropriate name when one watches the ocean as it hammers at the land there. Even now, late in the 20th century, to go to Brittany is to go back in time.

The tiny villages exist on fishing. The people's lives are of and by the sea and it is a very cruel sea there. The old women who move about the villages are all dressed in black. It is the black of mourning to honor the lost sons and husbands whom the sea has claimed. Brittany is a very Catholic land, endless masses are said in memory of their lost fishermen whose names are posted on long, sad lists in the churches.

The charm of Nantucket is of a different kind. It is a softer, gentler, landscape. The moors are like long rolling ocean swells. Their color changes with the seasons from green to gold to a kind of crisp, eye pleasing cranberry red then to a lonesome greyish-brown like the winter coats of the deer that live there. The beaches are a continuation of the easy pitch of the land, smooth, with grainy white sand that slopes to merge with the welcoming sea whose color has less dark ink than on the coast of France.

Storm waves seem to lose their harshness on Nantucket's mild shore. The Breton sea and landscape are convulsed and troubled. Nantucket is serene. The big storms of Brittany are unpredictable and erratic on the compass. They can rage from the North or West. The source of Nantucket weather is much more reliable, our big storms are Nor'easters.

But, of course, there are similarities and in the case of one of them my memory is stirred when I see the friendly yellow of Scotch Broom bushes on Nantucket because the same plant blooms with the same identical color in Brittany.

Like meeting a beautiful woman and learning that she also has great character and intelligence, I soon learned that Nantucket had much more than physical attraction. There is a special way of life that is here for those who take the trouble to reach out for it.

My learning about Nantucket living began on my first day. Earle MacAusland suggested we have clam chowder for lunch. When I told him I wasn't sure what clam chowder was, he was delighted rather than vexed.

"We'll go clamming and then come home and make a chowder," he said.

And we did.

After my first few useless probings with the clam rake, I dug up a clam and studied it as though it was a rock from the moon. My employer stood waist deep in the water and worked happily with his rake. Clearly this was an unusual man. When we returned to the house he showed me how to open the clams. The small ones were tangy and wonderful to taste. When I started to eat one of the big ones, he said, "No, no! We save those for chowder." I must have looked blankly at him because he said, "You really don't know clam chowder?"

I was concerned and I guess somewhat embarrassed to say I had never heard of it. He seemed pleased.

"Ahhh – I'll show you how it's done," he said. He led me through the steps of preparing New England Clam Chowder. Here is the way we did it.

Earle MacAusland's Clam Chowder

12 large quahogs (or 2 cups shucked meat)
½ pound salt pork, chopped
1 large onion, chopped
2 stalks celery, diced
1 cup milk
½ cup diced potatoes
1 bay leaf
1 sprig thyme
¼ cup heavy cream
2 ounces butter

If you use fresh quahogs, open them up, save the juice, remove the meat and chop it up coarsely, then put aside.

In a heavy-bottomed soup kettle, put the chopped salt pork and cook over medium heat for 5 minutes. Add the onions and sweat for 4 to 5 minutes. Then add the celery, the juice from the quahogs, the milk, the potatoes, bay leaf and thyme. Bring to a boil, then reduce the heat and simmer until the potatoes are soft – about 8 to 10 minutes.

Add the chopped quahogs and simmer for 5 more minutes. Add the cream, then bring to a boil, salt and pepper to taste, then finish by adding the butter just before serving.

It is fitting to begin with a recipe that I learned my first day on Nantucket, and it's especially right that the recipe comes from the man who had such an impact on dining in America. Long before Julia Child there was Earle MacAusland. He started *Gourmet*

Magazine with a small purse and a big dream. He told me his goal was for American women to spend more money in their kitchens than in their bathrooms.

Look around America and see for yourself how well he succeeded.

People told me that this American Scotchman who had achieved such spectacular success in business was a tough guy. I never saw it. We never had a harsh word or an unpleasant moment between us. The Nantucket natives said that he was practically a hermit, a recluse who lived on the edge of Polpis Harbor, drove into town every morning of the week in a Rolls Royce, picked up his *New York Times* and spoke to no one. My relationship with Earle MacAusland was one long series of lively, interesting conversations.

The fact is, we had similar views on the ingredients of the recipe for the good life. Earle MacAusland was certainly a water man. When we met he was in his seventies and some of his ability to do what he wanted was diminished, but his spirit in relating to nature remained intense. He had been an avid fisherman and owned a stretch of the Merrimishi River in Canada where the salmon fishing is superb. He was delighted that I loved to fish and he encouraged me to spend whatever time I wished on the water.

Earle MacAusland loved wild things and of all the animal kingdom he cared for ducks most. My knowledge of ducks came from the kitchen – I had cooked hundreds of them. Of live, wild ducks, I knew nothing. Nantucket changed all that. The world of game birds is a very important ingredient in my life now. It is another debt that I owe to Earle MacAusland.

Wild birds were his fascination – perhaps I should say his passion. He would sit in a lawn chair in good weather or in an easy chair inside if the weather was grim. He'd read and lift his head from time to time to watch his beloved birds. There were pintails, wood ducks, teal and many geese. He loved to attract a wide variety of birds. The more colorful, the more his pleasure. He once sent his private pilot to Alaska to pick up a pair of Chinese mandarin ducks. They were two beauties – two expensive beauties.

Some of these were pinioned ducks, birds whose wings were clipped so they could not fly away. But what a life those ducks led on beautiful Polpis Harbor. Everyday, rain or shine, one hundred pounds of corn were spread for the birds by the butler. That was a great sight – the uniformed butler spreading the corn for the birds. I'm sure Jean MacAusland was occasionally distressed by the deposits from the ducks on the lawn, but this inconvenience meant nothing to her husband.

Earle MacAusland's fascination with the beauty of birds infected me. I began to study the water fowl in minute detail – the curve of the neck, the sweep of the wings, the blend or contrast of the colors. One day a thought struck me and excited me. I knew how to sculpt. All chefs do. We prepare ice sculptures of all sizes and shapes. Unfortunately, that work ends up as a pool of water. I decided to try my hand at wood. Perhaps I could capture the beauty of these birds forever in wood.

I searched and bought a few basic tools. I began carving the image of a water fowl. It was 1973. In a sense, I have never stopped. Carving decoys and freestanding water fowl is one of my Nantucket winter pleasures. I am proud of my work and of the many blue ribbons I have won in national competitions, but I will never be more satisfied with my efforts than on the day I presented Earle MacAusland with my first accomplished carving – a male bufflehead duck.

The thought of shooting any of his flock's relatives was a horror to the boss. In fact, shooting any live thing was unpleasant to him. Mrs. MacAusland was fond of a rabbit dish that I prepare, so once in awhile she might point at the .22 rifle and quietly suggest that the rabbit stew would be a treat. I shot a few. It was my first game shooting and I found it challenging, but when the dish was served, the boss' reluctance to enjoy the food was obvious. From that time on we scheduled my rabbit-shot meals for occasions when he was away on magazine business.

Since that first beginning with the .22 and the rabbits I've spent endless happy hours tramping Nantucket's moors watching my dogs work to find me a pheasant for our dinner table, and there have been even longer hours in my little camouflaged aluminum boat or shivering in a blind waiting for a shot at a duck that I know will taste so good on our table. Some people find it puzzling and strange that I have become a wild fowl conservationist and a carver of these birds and yet I shoot them. Maybe it seems a contradiction, but to me – a Frenchman – it is logical. If you don't work to protect and increase the birds, there won't be any to shoot for your dinner table. To me that is clear.

To Earle MacAusland, however, that was unacceptable. He wanted all of the birds protected on his island, and I think maybe he thought of it that way – his island. How he loved Nantucket! He hated to leave.

I used to have lots of secret chuckles watching him when the time came to go "off island." He was like a kid on those days. He would appear in the kitchen early in the morning dressed for the city – impeccable in a three-piece suit. He would pace up and down, peering out the window, up at the sky, tapping and analysing the barometer.

"Well," he would say and depending on the season, it would be, "perhaps it will rain," – or snow – or be foggy.

He was a schoolboy hoping that something, anything providential would occur to keep him from the clutches of his schoolroom, which for him was the city.

As it is for many of us, Nantucket was a special magnet for him and it is very hard to pull away.

I believe as time went on, Earle MacAusland was more comfortable with his beloved ducks than he was with crowds of people. He definitely was not a man for the cocktail party circuit, but the MacAuslands did enjoy hosting small dinner parties. These provided three of the things they treasured most – exciting food, memorable wine, and thoughtful conversation.

In the tradition that is so rigorously upheld by his superb magazine, any meal at the MacAuslands was an occasion and I hope, a treat. The evening meal was always an event. Guests or not, Mr. and Mrs. MacAusland dressed for dinner and were served formally by the butler.

For Anne and me, Sunday meals with the MacAuslands will always shine brightly in our memories. It was not what we expected to find in America. Sunday lunch in France is the meal of the week – even the most humble family goes out to eat on occassion. Where ever it's taken, the meal lasts all afternoon. It is a warm tradition that in many ways is unique.

Earle MacAusland went one step further. In the house overlooking Polpis Harbor on

Nantucket the Sunday meal was a ceremony. Anne and Marc were always invited. There were a couple of reasons for this. The first was the natural courtesy of the MacAuslands. The second was the fact Anne was a Scot! As I look back, I suppose Anne and I were the perfect combination for Earle MacAusland – a French chef with a Scotch wife.

Earle MacAusland had the greatest respect for French cuisine. *Gourmet Magazine* still reflects that respect. That was his public and professional side. More intense and very private was his pride in his Scottish heritage. On Sunday the MacAusland blood was celebrated. I always tried to make the meal the grandest of the week. Often I would work late Saturday, sometimes until three or four in the morning, go to Mass early Sunday morning and then rush out to Polpis. The MacAuslands' Rolls, with the boss himself at the controls would pick up Anne and Marc from the house we rented in town. Mrs. MacAusland would meet them at the door with great courtesy. Earle always wore his kilt with the family plaid. Occasionally, the house would be filled with the sound of recorded bagpipe tunes. I always wanted to have the meal match all of this. That's why Sunday was a great day. My family and the MacAuslands at the table being served food that I produced in the kitchen. I could look out the window and there was the ocean. There were no waiters screaming. I didn't have to yell. Everything was calm. I could cook each dish to perfection. It was like heaven.

For me this all proved to be a marvelous opportunity to test and refine my professional skills. Charles Barrier had worked for a number of years for a private family before becoming Chef de Cuisine. I knew he considered that time well spent. He was right as usual. I found it to be an opportunity for professional enrichment. I could experiment to test the boundaries of my most esoteric food fantasies, and I had two discriminating palates to respond to my adventures in the kitchen. My head was full of the challenge of cooking. I would get up at six and begin my projects. No one asked me to. I had to. There was so much I wanted to try or to improve. Oftentimes I would still be in the kitchen at midnight. The list in my head seemed endless, as was my pleasure at having my efforts well received. Foie gras, truffles, any special food item that I requested was gotten for me – and quickly. Just send the plane. It was amazing.

Meats and stews, special sauces, desserts of every kind, fish dishes were always welcome. I dammed a small brook on the property and raised pickerel and trout. The Boston Whaler and the beautiful old *Malahini* were there for me to use at any time, either for my pleasure or to fish for the table.

These were the days before the decimation of the striped bass population, and I slowly learned some of the magic of fishing for those splendid fish. I met a Nantucket native and salt water fishing genius, Bob Francis, who completed my education. Apparently too many of us learned those lessons because the fish is now a threatened species. I will not serve it at the Chanticleer even if someone brings me a legal size striper. I believe that restaurants saying "no way" on serving striped bass is a small but helpful way to try and preserve and restore that great fish.

Along with the bass of course there was – and is – the bluefish. Savage and, I would guess, indestructible. It is everyman's saltwater game fish. All you need is a place to stand – beach, dock, bridge. When the blues are feeding all you need to do is put a plug in the water. They will strike anything. Cut the end off a broom handle and fix a hook in it – no need to be fancy. The bluefish will attack the movement in the water. They are voracious feeders, so much so that once full they will go to the bottom and bounce on the ocean floor to disgorge their food so they can eat again. This is the reason that an oily slick appears on the surface of the water where a school of blues is feeding. These slicks are strong enough that you can smell them. I always have wondered what would happen if a person fell overboard into a school of hungry blues.

It took me a couple of stitches to learn that after you catch the bluefish you must be careful that he doesn't catch you. They will snap and bite and tear with their dying breath.

No doubt about it, the bluefish is the blue-collar game fish all along the East Coast of America. But there is one more catch to this fish. It is so oily and strong that it tends to be overpowering as a meal. It is extremely difficult to make into a delicate or subtle dish. When I was serving the MacAuslands, it was not a fish that was looked for on their table.

I have experimented with cooking bluefish since I discovered Nantucket. I've tasted the basic recipes that the natives use to cut the strength of the fish, which generally means covering the fish with mayonnaise and chopped onion or stewed tomatoes. To me that is camouflage, not cooking. I experimented with many approaches. I even used the fish in a quenelle. Nothing pleased me. But I knew I must persevere. It seemed to me that the bluefish was the perfect challenge for a French chef. People think of French food as being rich and elegant, or perhaps precise and subtle. Certainly that is the sort of description that we strive for, but one should not forget what French cooking is all about – its origin, its purpose. French cooking was not an art developed to please the rich. French cuisine evolved from the wish or perhaps more accurately, the need to take the most common food, the most basic items on a peasant's table and make them tasty and tastier and tastier.

More accessible than cod, bluefish is the common fish of Nantucket. Yet, it is not eagerly eaten. This was where my years of training could be decisive. I continued to seek the right ingredients that would combine with the flavor and strength of the fish into a reliable and memorable dish.

At long last I found what I searched for! A truly great recipe for bluefish. If you visit the ocean, even if you hate fishing, you probably know the fishermen generally can hardly give away the bluefish they catch so easily. Now, take one, or pay the going rate – which is usually only five or ten cents a pound – and create a tasty dish that is also a great bargain. Even if you hate the taste of bluefish you should try my approach. I promise you a delightful surprise, a most unusual dish. After all my experimenting it finally came to me to use some of my North African experience. One of the things I learned there is that the French aren't alone in appreciating good food and in turning what might be called a peasant's dish into a delicacy. Every culture has methods of food preparation that are unique. Bluefish Timgad is a surprising reward from my time in the Algerian War.

How good is it? Even Nantucket folks who tell me they usually can't stand the strength of the bluefish come out to the Chanticleer and order it over and over again. Often they tell me, with a touch of embarrassment, that they have come out "just to have the bluefish." Of course, I'm delighted.

I urge you to try this terrific recipe for Bluefish Timgad. You'll find the recipe on page 127. I wish Earle MacAusland was here to taste this creation. I think he'd be surprised and, I hope, delighted.

Perhaps you are wondering what Timgad means. Well, it is an Arab word that is also the name of a fine Moroccan restaurant in Paris. The chef is a fellow I like to have a drink with. Since the bluefish recipe came to my mind while thinking of the way fish is done in North Africa, I decided to honor my friend and his restaurant by giving the bluefish the name Timgad. I have no idea what it actually means! I must ask my friend the next time I sit at his table in Paris.

The three year contract with Earle MacAusland was coming to a close and although it would be painful, I knew I must move on. We had had the best of everything, thoughtful, caring employers in a place that we were growing to love. Strange, I am an outdoor, active person. Anne is not, yet she was as taken with Nantucket life as I. It was what we were both looking for even though we didn't know it until we found it. Still, I didn't see how we could stay on the Island. There was nothing for us to have as our own.

Any number of times I would say to myself before falling asleep, "I must tell Earle tomorrow that we are going to leave." In the morning I would postpone. I hated to do it. We were such good friends. Finally, though, it had to happen.

Of course, Earle MacAusland was a gentleman. He said, "What do you want to do? Where do you want to go? I will help in any way I can."

I didn't know. The idea of going back to France was growing very faint. I know now that's what happens. America is so seductive. We immigrants, we leave for America, we say we'll stay two or three years then we will come back. America is too good to leave. Just ask my friend Lucien. He came from Belgium to cook at the Opera House on Nantucket for a summer. Thirty years later he was still there.

So, we decided we would look around America. We went to Rhinebeck, New York and looked at an old inn. George Washington had slept there. It was a nice place. I could see the potential. The owner wanted to work out a lease-purchase arrangement, but we couldn't get anything serious down on paper.

Then we had some more luck. This time it was orchestrated by someone who believed in us and reached out to help. Her name is Pat Pullman. Pat lives here on the island and is still one of our greatest boosters. Pat helped us by using that strange social event called the cocktail party. Don't ever believe that those events have to be a waste of time. Sometimes an encounter over a drink can change your life. For us there were two occasions when Pat gave us a helping hand. The second time would decide our destiny.

First she introduced us to Parmelia Reed. This caused us to go to Florida for two winters while I cooked at the Jupiter Island Club at Hobe Sound which the Reeds owned. I wouldn't be surprised if the Hobe Sound Colony is the quietest concentration of money and power in America. Those were two interesting winters for a couple of French immigrants and their little baby boy. That was from one Nantucket cocktail party.

Our summers were still on Nantucket. You see, we really didn't want to leave. So far all of our American summers have been on Nantucket. I hope they will always be.

This is where the second important cocktail was drunk.

I was walking around at this party in 'Sconset not knowing if the Jupiter Island job was going to happen. Pat grabbed me by the arm and said, "There is someone I want you to meet. She's got a story you should listen to."

So, Pat introduced me to a woman named Topsy and says she is Roy Larsen's daughter. I know about him. He is the chairman of Time-Life and a fierce protector of what is good about Nantucket and especially the village of 'Sconset. Topsy tells me that her father and some 'Sconset friends have just bought the Chanticleer Restaurant in the village because they were afraid someone was going to turn it into a pizza parlor and they want a first class restaurant in 'Sconset. I understood that because I had learned by then that the 'Sconset people would be happy if they never had to go into Nantucket Town. She tells me these guys are like a bunch of Indians without a chief.

So it was arranged that I would meet with these Indians, and quite a tribe they were. The late Roy Larsen, John Rhodes, Bill Matteson, Doctor Jerome Dickenson and Peter Heller. All Sconseters – by that I mean they all had homes in Siasconset which is an Indian word that has been shortened to 'Sconset. It is a small village on the Eastern edge of Nantucket. This is where our restaurant, the Chanticleer, was created as a small inn in 1909.

I guess you could say codfish created 'Sconset. This fish used to be in great abundance in the rips that work not far from the beach. What is a rip? I had to learn that too. It is a place of ocean turbulence that usually produces breaking waves and perhaps white water. I think it is caused by a sharp unevenness on the ocean floor or by two wave currents hitting into one another. Fish get turned about in a rip, so the bigger fish work the edges, snapping up the smaller ones – just like life.

Beginning in the 1600's the Indians got moved out as Nantucketers built little wooden shacks along the bluff and on the beach so they could stay close to this source of fish. I admit prejudice, but I think 'Sconset – with its little wooden cottages shoulder to shoulder and narrow twisting lanes – is one of the prettiest, most unique places I have ever seen. So did this band of modern Indians who called themselves 'Sconset Enterprises. They were truly concerned about the Chanticleer as an important part of their village. They wanted a first class restaurant in 'Sconset mostly because, like all true 'Sconseters, they wanted nothing to do with driving into Nantucket Town to go out to dinner. 'Sconset people see their village as the most special place within the specialness that is Nantucket. Amazing, eh? But – they are right.

The 'Sconset Enterprise men had hired a woman to be the front of the house manager. It was agreed that I would run the kitchen and that while I was working in Florida the young woman would spend the winter getting the Chanticleer shaped up for the summer season.

When our season in Florida was over we hurried back to Nantucket, and I tell you, we couldn't wait to get back.

We were dismayed at what we found at the Chanticleer. It was a shambles. The girl had had a fun winter living in the building and using the company car, but the place was in worse shape than when we left – nothing clean or orderly. The interior of the building actually looked as though it had been trashed.

I got in touch with the 'Sconset Indians and told them they had better have one boss and it better be somebody responsible. So, the lady manager of the front of the house was gone. I became their chef/manager.

So, we began. We had increased our family – a beautiful little girl we named Nathalie. Anne had her hands full at home. There was no time for restaurants for her in those days. 1970 was our first year and there was a hell of a lot of hard work and no profit. We went back to the Jupiter Island Club that winter. We had to – we had no money. For the next two years I spent summers working for the 'Sconset investors and winters in the kitchen at Hobe Sound. In some areas I felt we weren't making progress. We were still renting in Nantucket and living in the help's quarters in Florida – living out of suitcases with two little children.

We decided to see if we could buy a house on Nantucket. We were truly hooked by then. We both knew it was where we wanted to be. We saw a house on Westchester Street in Nantucket Town that we could make the mortgage payments on if we could find the money for a down payment.

There was one person I knew I could turn to. I went to Earle MacAusland and told him what we were trying to do. I asked him if he would loan me ten thousand dollars. Mon Dieu! I hated to ask but we understood one another so well. Without hesitating he wrote out the check.

"Of course, there will be no interest charged," he said, "and pay it off when you can."

What a man! What a friend!

That was the start. A year after that the Chanticleer owners offered to sell me the restaurant at a price I couldn't refuse. I remortgaged the house on Westchester Street. That is where the Chanticleer money came from. That group of Indians proved in their pocketbook how committed they were to 'Sconset. They said they never intended to be restaurateurs, but they wanted a place in 'Sconset they could be proud of. They said that if I would promise to stay committed to the Chanticleer for a reasonable time I could buy it at this oh-so-fair price because they believed in my ability to create a noteworthy restaurant. I believe I have done that and I want it to be put on paper how much I appreciate that they gave me the chance. Truly the chance of a lifetime. Ahhh! What a country America is, and what a combination – Nantucket and the Chanticleer!

I knew the Chanticleer could be the keystone of our life. The basic, the foundation – like the *fond* is for creating a delicious dish. And so it is. But first, and always, there must be hard work.

The first couple of years as owners I spent the winter in Nantucket as a scallop fisherman. This way we could earn some money and spend the rest of each day working on fixing things at the restaurant. There was plenty to do.

Scalloping is Nantucket's winter cash crop. Beginning on the first Monday of November, when the first light comes, you will see a flotilla of small boats making slow, steady circles in the water in the town harbour, in Polpis or off Madaket and Tuckernuck. The boats are towing steel ringed dredges along the bottom. If you stand and watch a while you will see Nantucket men and women hauling up heavy loads of seaweed and kelp and dumping them on flat culling boards that are built in the midsection of the boats. From these piles of ocean growth they sort out the scallops that Nantucket waters have always had in special abundance. By now you know I am prejudiced but if you try some I think you will agree that Nantucket Bay scallops are the best you have ever tasted. The fact that the ocean provides them just for the taking has always seemed to me to be a kind of minor miracle.

The two winters after scalloping I spent as a chef at the Colony Hotel in Palm Beach. The money was better than fishing and we needed it. There were plenty of things to spend it on in the restaurant. Like all old things, the building needs lots of attention.

These days there isn't as much to be done in the restaurant in the winter, so Anne and I take a couple of weeks to go to the sun. But the rest of our winter we spend right here – on-island. Funny about that word – winter. We hear it often from off-island people in the summer. When it occurs there is a set pattern to the conversation. Here's the way it goes:

"Do you live here on the island year round?"

"Yes."

"Really! What's it like in the winter?"

That is the guaranteed second question.

For Anne and me what it's like in the winter is easy, friendly and slow. Nobody gets excited. The rare snowstorms are welcomed by the children and photographers, tolerated and probably secretly enjoyed by the rest of us who measure it against our memories of past storms. There are no traffic jams, but there might be some jammed kitchens with people finding the weather a good excuse for an impromptu party. In fact, winter is the time the Berruets do their personal partying and we get even for social time lost in the summer.

From time to time during the winter I conduct a small, informal cooking class with some lady friends. This gathering always results in a very pleasant lunch with a perfect mix of food, wine, and off season gossip.

During the shooting season I am in a duck blind when the sun gets up or I am tramping the moors with one of my dogs. The rest of my mornings are spent testing new recipies that will be on the Chanticleer's menu for the coming year.

The afternoons are saved for wood carving. Put it all together and it's a time for thoughtful but busy living.

So, when people ask the predictable question about winter, the Nantucketers just shrug because we don't want everybody to know that winter on Nantucket is wonderful!

Anne came to work at the Chanticleer after the second year. I needed someone to be my eyes and my voice when I should have been elsewhere but had to be at the stove. It works just that way. The Chanticleer is our place – we are very much partners. I couldn't do my thing there without her. She runs the front of the house and she is superb. She doesn't miss a thing. The silverware, the crystal, the china, all immaculate and correctly placed. The linen smooth, the flowers fresh and exquisitely arranged, the pictures hung correctly. Anne has the eye for detail. If there is a flaw, she will rectify it. She also keeps an eagle eye on the waiters; if she sees one of them out-of-line she'll set that straight. Anne has a rule for people who don't frequently visit elegant restaurants: Never, ever be intimidated by the waiter.

Partnerships in the restaurant business are very tricky. They mostly fail. One person cooks, the other runs the front. The guy in the kitchen says, "Son of a bitch, I'm covered with sweat, and here's my partner floating around in his tuxedo smiling at the ladies, patting the big shot millionaires' shoulders, what the hell am I doing baking myself in this kitchen all night?" Even if it's two chefs who try it, one has to be boss and the thing falls apart.

With a husband and wife, there is no question of this. No problem. Everyone knows the wife is the boss.

In European restaurants it is usual to see a husband and wife team. Not so in America, but I think you will see it more and more. It works. You'll agree if you watch Anne move around the tables at the Chanticleer. It's under control. The kitchen and the front of the house are two different worlds. In one are the cooks, in the other the waiters. It's like totally different countries on the same planet. In France the young cooks rode bicycles, the waiters drove cars. In America the same proportions hold true. It's the same everywhere. I remember some years ago being asked to take a job as chef at a famous Tokyo hotel. It was an old French chef who was retiring and going back home who tried to recruit me. As we talked he growled, "It's the same there. The waiters make a ton of money off the sweat of our brow."

In a place like Nantucket the tips are big, so the waiters make even more money. But like everywhere else, very few of them ever keep any of it. Why? I don't know but they never have any money. They spend it all. It's all cash – perhaps that's the problem. They blow two hundred dollars, shrug, and tell you they can make it the next night. Of course, this drives the kitchen workers crazy and I don't blame them. So, when we have a party of twenty or more, I keep 50% of the tip for the kitchen fund and split it between these guys. They see a little bit of extra money from this and that makes them feel a little better.

More important than that, however, is the comradeship of the kitchen. We have our traditional Saturday night champagne drinking. They like that – I like that. We sit, drink and discuss the week we have had. Sometimes we drink too much because our spirits are high. It's like a happy family. My friend, K.C. Jones, coach of the Boston Celtics, has told me he believes the best teams in basketball are like families, and you have to work to create that feeling. That's the way we are in the kitchen at the Chanticleer. We work together, we know the team comes first. I have always had great kids on my team. They have been great team players and I think our restaurant reflects that.

One of the French kings, it was Louis the XIV, said, "L'etat c'est moi" – I am the state. Historians think of that as being rather arrogant, but the fact is that it was true. He was the state and, without arrogance I would say – and I think my partner agrees with me – I am the Chanticleer.

Perhaps you would like to know what is involved in a day in the life of the Chanticleer.

Let's go through an August day. They are always busy days.

At 6:45 in the morning I am into the shower.

By 7:15 I am on the Polpis Road on my way to work. Often a couple of the kitchen guys will be living at Hollywood Farm and I stop to pick them up. Probably a few mallards are in the little pond there. For a second or two I watch them cruise across the still, unrippled surface of the pond or stand at the water's edge, preening their feathers. Even without ducks the Nantucket ponds are special.

We proceed along the road. There is seldom any traffic at that time. Perhaps a couple of cyclists – some young fellow and one of the stunning women who come to the island. I hope they are lovers.

I slow down to look at Sasaccacha Pond and I take a nice deep breath and smell the sea through the open window of the car. Some adventurous early rising summer visitor might be sailing a little Sunfish on the pond. The morning sun paints the colors of the sky and the sea and the sail with that special tone that the Impressionists seem to catch and is so much part of the soft color scheme of our island.

At 7:30 we are in the kitchen ready to work. I expect everybody to be here by 7:45 and they are. Very seldom is anyone late. The baker is already at work since he begins at 3:00 or 4:00 in the morning. He is independent, does his own thing – but, of course, I peek over his shoulder.

7:45 – Everybody is in the kitchen. I start the day with a cup of coffee and conversation with the sous chef and the third chef about the two phases of the day. Lunch and dinner are two different menus. We talk of that and whatever specials I might be planning for lunch or dinner. We check to see if there is a private party and if so, what have they chosen.

A lot of chefs don't spend much time at the stove anymore or even in the kitchen. Many have an office off the kitchen and they stay there. They give their ideas to the sous chef and he is the sergeant major. He is in charge of discipline, schedule and overseeing the plan of the day. That is not the way it is at the Chanticleer. I make the plan and then everybody starts working – all of us.

Each underchef has his own station. There is a guy taking care of the fish, one taking care of meat, one vegetables, one salad and, of course, one is doing sauces and he is busy right from the start preparing stock. In the spring when I have the restaurant prepared for the season I have a photograph made showing the layout that I want at each station with all the tools and basic ingredients arranged in a specific manner. Each station will look like the photograph because that photo is pasted up right over the station. Prepping is done at each one for both luncheon and dinner starting in the morning.

8:00 – Now I get on the phone and talk to the purveyors. I want fresh fish every day. I get what I can in Nantucket, but as the years go on, Nantucket has fewer and fewer fishermen and more and more carpenters. Consequently, I do a lot of business with Chatham fishermen and fish wholesalers on Cape Cod. They put the morning catch of fish on a plane to me and I have it for noon. There is one fellow in Chatham who traps sea bass. He is in by 9:00 or 10:00 every morning and by noon the fish are on the plane to me. These fish are beautiful, you wouldn't believe – right out of the water. If I can't find grey sole on Nantucket I get it flown over from Chatham too. After the fish is ordered, I talk to my meat seller in Boston. We get fresh meat three times a week. However, if I need something special for that day's menu, it will be airfreighted down. The same with vegetables.

I spend an hour on the phone in the morning just talking to people to make sure we have the right fresh products on hand for the day.

This is something that I have thought a lot about. Too many products are imported to our island. Particularly too many food products. I have a goal to make the Chanticleer, I guess you would say, "Nantucket sufficient." Curiously, in a way this all began with ducks. I belong to an organization called Ducks Unlimited. Some people misunderstand this organization. Basically it is a conservation group comprised of both hunters and bird lovers who raise large sums of money to keep space and environmental conditions healthy for ducks. Nantucket is one of the leading money raising spots of its size for Ducks Unlimited. One of our members is a young fellow named Stephen Swift – a great guy, very exceptional. He makes elegant furniture by hand and is considered a leading American craftsman. One night Stephen and I got talking at a Ducks Unlimited dinner and he told me he was raising some quail to use in dog training.

I said, "How about raising some for the restaurant and some pheasants?" I promised that I would buy everything that he raised the first year. So he did and I did and it went very well. It was obvious that he fed them nothing but the best. That's the way Steve operates. So, I said to him, "Let's do ducks," and that was the beginning. Now he furnishes all our fowl. He and I are experimenting on crossbreeding mallards with muscovy ducks to produce a fleshier bird. Stephen Swift has God knows how many birds now and supplies restaurants all over the East Coast.

Nantucket grows fine vegetables in the summer but I would like to improve the situation. I am working with a fellow named Bill Broughton right in 'Sconset. I get a lot of my vegetables from him and every year I ask him to grow one more thing. He has ruby red lettuce that is the best I have ever seen. Beautiful, like a flower they are so red. He is doing French green beans for me now. They are really tender and succulent. The other island farms also have great vegetables. I don't like to buy any from off-island if I can help it.

There was a woman in Vermont raising sheep. They were perfect, but the problem, as usual, was with the airplanes. You can't have fresh lamb sitting in an airport. Now I am talking with a girl who is going to try and raise some sheep here on this island, which of course used to be covered with sheep. I hope she does it.

Nantucket has shellfish – and oysters in particular we have like nobody else in the world. You wouldn't believe what these oysters taste like until you have one in your mouth. About four years ago some Nantucket fellows started farming these oysters in Polpis Harbor. In that short time they have brought out of the water a bit of food that has no equal anywhere, and I include my native Brittany when I say that.

There's one item that I use in my recipes that I never have to worry about being available – cranberries. We have a bounty of them. In fact, I have always been told that the great bog in the middle of the island is the largest single cranberry bog in America.

There are hazelnuts in the woods here. I know a place where I find them sprinkled in a beautiful bed of Indian Slippers. I get them every year and use them. Sweet blueberries and beach plums are also here for the picking.

In certain salt marshes there is a seaweed that the French call *pourpier.* I use it as a vegetable with poached fish. It is delicious and full of nutrition. Believe it or not, I used to buy it from a New York market that got it from a Paris distributor who got it from "a special place in Brittany." What irony! Now I find it right here in Madaket harbor. Maybe pourpier followed Berruet from Brittany to Nantucket.

It's all here – you have to look. The raspberries that you get at the Chanticleer and the herbs we use don't have to travel very far. I raise them in the backyard of the restaurant.

Beef and veal – well, I don't have that settled yet but I am thinking about it.

If you ask me sometime in the future what the day at the Chanticleer is like, I hope I'll tell you I'm be spending less time on long distance phone calls ordering food.

9:00 – The salesmen start coming in. I talk with them. I buy everything for the restaurant. No one else can order or buy anything. This is my way to conrol the entire operation. I know what we need, what comes in, and what is going out. I talk to the salesmen and at the same time I begin working at the stove. There are certain dishes that I do myself. So, the salesman stands there in the kitchen while I work at the stove and we talk. That is the only way I know how to do it. I get interrupted with a million questions and the telephone, but that's things happening at the Chanticleer.

10:00 – The waiters come in. I talk with Tracy, our maitre d', about the plans for the day – who has made reservations and where they like to sit and that Mr. So-and-So called and wants two bottles of an old Bordeaux pulled out of the cellar, also So-and-So and So-and-So have made reservations, they like a particular kind of wine. We'll take some of these wines from the cellar and settle them down so that they are at room temperature.

The people of the Chanticleer know they can interrupt me at any time to discuss wine. They know that wine is a very special passion in my life and I suppose they understand that I believe that a meal without wine is like a world without color. I am very proud of the Chanticleer's wine cellar. We have received many awards for the quality of our inventory. Recently we were presented with the Grand Award of Excellence by *The Wine Spectator,* America's premier wine magazine. This award signifies that we have one of the outstanding wine lists in the world. I like to think of the Chanticleer's wine cellar as the equivalent of a great library. We have over 10,000 volumes in our library, some of which we won't think about enjoying for five or even ten years when they are just right for tasting. When I walk in and touch those bottles I can't believe this is the same kid who swiped that bottle of Clos Vougeot from his father all those long years ago.

But now on this August morning, there is no time for daydreaming. My secretary, Lorna, comes in and while I am stirring the frying pan we discuss correspondence that needs to be dealt with.

11:00 – A quick lunch on the move. There is no time to sit down. We eat a bowl of soup or a sandwich as we go. We set up for our luncheon clients. I have a crew that does lunch and one that does dinner. At 12:00, the dinner crew leaves. Meanwhile, we are getting the lunch ready. The range has to be cleared of all sauces and any specialty items that are being prepped for dinner. This must be done by 11:30 so that we have room to work the luncheon meal. I do lunch because I like to do it.

In France the pressure in the kitchen is different because it is one menu and everybody works lunch and dinner. Here, lunch has traditionally been a much lighter meal, but it is starting to change. People are getting very serious with lunch. I do lunch everyday because I don't want lunch to be a second-rate meal. My presence means everybody pays attention. The waiters don't take it lightly; they know I want things to be just as right as at dinner time and it's working out that way. We have a small but good lunch business.

12:00 – First customers come in. We go on from there until 2:30.

The clean up man works from 2:30 until 4:00. I go talk to Mrs. Gibbs who handles our reservations, then with Lorna to see if there is any problem with our paperwork and then I try to read the paper and see if there is any news of the Celtics. I keep a cot in a small room beside my office and I will stretch out and try and take a catnap.

4:00 – We go back to work. The dinner crew that left at 12:00 is back. The lunch crew will return at 6:00 so they have had a four hour break too.

We start the final tune-up to get everything ready for the night. I go through the sauces for the night, the soups, I taste-test things. I make sure absolutely everything is O.K.

We do the bases in the morning and then we finalize things at 4:00. So from 4:00 to 5:00 that is what we do – make sure we have everything ready. I check every station to make sure they are fully prepared. I learned when I was a paratrooper that if you don't check things carefully you will fall on your ass. At this time I am making sure the Chanticleer doesn't fall on its ass.

5:00 – Dinner. We all eat. We take one full hour and that is important. We must have dinner and a glass of wine or two. It's very important. We feed everybody well. We do not use leftovers. I have one person whose sole job is to cook the employees' meals. You can't give your people second rate food to eat and expect them to work well. They are going to be serving fine food, I want them to be fed the same way. After all, we are in the restaurant business.

We have a good time – good laughs. We don't talk about work. We talk about fishing, women, sports, people, whatever – but no work.

6:00 – The final battle plan. Everybody goes through their setups again to make sure every item is there. I check them all.

I go into the dinning room and talk to the waiters for a half hour. We talk about particular wines that work well with various dishes. I explain how we are preparing a certain dish. I ask if they have any questions about the menu. I tell them if we are out of something. But basically our conversation is of the menu and the wines. Of course, if there was a mistake the day before, we talk about it.

6:30 – Anne comes in and checks the dinning rooms, table settings, everything the client is going to see. We both know how we want that to be. She has a great sense of the place.

7:00 – The first customer is seated. We keep moving at a steady pace until 10:30. There is no food warming or sitting. Each item is cooked individually for the plate. We try to deal with an order every ten or fifteen minutes. The last reservation is usually for 10:00 and at 10:30 we put out our last meal. It is pretty steady. There are occasions, I know, when people feel their food is slow in arriving. When this happens, however, it is not because we are lazy; it's because the dish is being individually prepared.

By 10:30 we start cleaning the kitchen. I have a guy wash the floor and the walls during the night, but we take care of the range and the tables and equipment. People come and say, "I can't believe it's so clean," but it has to be. You can't cook good food with a dirty kitchen. The guys have to look clean too. I don't care how many times they change their uniform – I pay for them so they better be clean.

11:30 – We are done cleaning and sit down at the table to have a glass of champagne or beer – whatever they want. We make a list of things we have to do tomorrow. By then it is midnight and I might go talk to a few people in the bar. If some close friends are there I might have a little wine with them, but I don't socialize too much in the dining room because if I do people might be offended if I spend time with some and not with others. It can get touchy and we are not in business to offend our clients.

Once in awhile, however, there might be a special reason to spend time in the dining room. One occasion was a few years ago when Jack Warner was entertaining a dear pal of his who is an Englishman, a former professional soldier who was a World War II commander of a parachute battalion. Now in civilian life, he is an engineer and a wine grower. This man's name is Sam Roughton and he grows Muller Thurgau grapes in a vineyard on his property, in a little village outside of Bath, that produce a very nice Reisling table wine. Earlier in the day that they were having dinner at the Chanticleer, Jack brought a bottle of Sam Roughton's wine out to the restaurant. When the Warner party arrived they were seated with lots of appropriate curtseying by Anne and bowing and scraping by Tracy and a couple of waiters. All very formal. Jack called for the wine list. He then indicated that there was no wine of sufficient grandeur on our wine list that was fitting for his friend. He ordered Tracy, who was party to this charade, to produce the chef. I was waiting in the wings, of course. When I came to the table Sam Roughton was leafing through our wine book. He looked at me and said, "I don't think I have ever seen a finer assortment of wines offered anywhere."

As I mumbled my thanks, Jack insisted that I must have some really grand bottle of wine, something better than what was listed, something really special that I had kept off the list. I finally admitted that there was one but that the price was astronomical.

"How much?" he asked and I quoted a figure that caused Roughton to rock back in his chair.

"Bring it," Jack ordered. Sam Roughton stared at his pal with that special look Europeans give Americans when they think they are acting especially wild. I motioned to Tracy and he came back with a wicker wine basket that he reverently offered to the host for inspection. He asked his English friend if he would like to take a look at the bottle.

"By God, I would," he said eagerly.

The table broke into whoops of laughter at the sound of Sam Roughton's yelp of surprise when he peered into the wicker and spied the bottle of Roughton's United Kingdom Dry White Table Wine.

For a good laugh like that, I'll always come out of the kitchen.

Saturday night when we finish I bring out the champagne and we of the kitchen crew sit like family and relax and drink. That's another time for laughs.

Other nights I get home about 1:00 and watch the news or read for a bit. You go to sleep fast because 6:00 is right around the corner. That's my day. That's a Chanticleer day. A full day – a busy day – a rewarding day. That's the way it is every day from May until October.

There are couple of things that break this pattern and they have also become part of my life with the Chanticleer.

In the spring when the Boston Celtics are in the play-offs – and I hope they always will be – I bring a radio into the kitchen and we listen to Johnny Most announce the games. If you don't know anything about basketball or even if you hate the game, try listening to Johnny Most just once. His voice and enthusiasm make his broadcasting a special dish, one you won't forget. On play-off game nights we shut the stoves off at 9:30 – no exceptions. Then all of us, the whole kitchen gang, we drop everything and rush into my back office and watch the last of the game on TV. Sometimes it seems to be a different game than the one Mr. Most was announcing.

The cleanup man earns his money during the play-offs because we really do drop everything and rush to watch those games.

The other break in my routine is Wednesday which is the closed day for the Chanticleer and the open day for me.

Wednesday mornings I rejoice because that's the day I go fishing. Off-shore, as we say in Nantucket.

I have a twenty-eight foot open boat and unless the weather is bad enough to make the seagulls walk, I head out to sea Wednesday morning. I often have my friend Bob Ruley with me. He is a native born Nantucketer who knows his way around the ocean like no one else. Of course you have got to pay attention to Ruley's instructions when he tells you where to find the fish. I asked him one day how to find a special fishing spot that he had taken me to, a place more than twenty miles off the coast of the island. "Just follow each buoy from one horizon to the next," he said. "When you don't see another buoy, you're there." Those are real Nantucket fishing instructions!

What I catch on Wednesday I cook for our clients on Thursday. I hope they get as much pleasure tasting those fish as I do catching them and cooking them, and I hope all of you have as much pleasure earning your living as Jean-Charles Berruet does.

Nantucket has made it possible for me to fulfill my dreams. We have a restaurant that any French chef might envy. I cherish the time spent in preparing food in the best possible way we can and giving people a chance to drink the finest French and American wines – and by the way, we Americans are producing some wonderful wines.

I tell you right now, in the off season, during all the winter days, no matter how much fun I am having, I miss being in the Chanticleer. I wish the restaurant was open. It is a joy to me when I am there.

I guess you know by now why it is that often when I raise my glass of wine, I make the silent toast, "Here's to Nantucket."

A Nantucket super-byway.

In Europe these would be shacks for the poorest of the poor –
Nantucket is a long way from Europe.

Just a back lane in 'Sconset!

Some of us work and some of us play, but no one is wasting time.

The ocean and this beach have an everlasting love affair.

Some of the Nantucket scallop fleet at work on a winter morning.

And this is a bit of their harvest – the best tasting scallops in the world.

A Nantucket day begins.

I wish Monet or Renoir had visited Nantucket.

*The Scotch broom reminds me of my native Brittany,
but the windmill reminds me of where I want to be.*

A last splash of color to warm us through the grey winter.

It's hard to say which one of us enjoys these mornings more.

Almost real!

A look at heaven.

Bluefish Timgad – a sublime ending for a savage fish.

If this old-timer could talk, we'd hear lots of Nantucket gossip.

Salt air, flowers, fog, and weathered shingles –
a recipe for a memorable walk.

You can see why this is one of my favorite spots in Polpis Harbor.

Bogged down in cranberries.

*Here are some other Nantucket beauties that you'll see on Main Street
and on the table at the Chanticleer.*

*These ripe beach plums will be made into a sauce that
is my favorite to serve with game birds. They give the
dish a wonderful fresh essence of the outdoors.*

We're becoming an American institution.

The Chanticleer's outdoor dining area. If you listen carefully, you might here the pop of a Champagne cork and a gentle laugh.

I am not the State, the Town of Nantucket, or the Village of 'Sconset – but I am the Chanticleer.

The Chanticleer's kitchen team – ready for another season.

*I guess this is what the big executives mean by
hands-on management.*

I like my teammates to keep everything in order.

*These are some of the glorious riches of France
that rest in our wine cellar.*

*Some of California's best – and they are getting
better all the time.*

I think the camera made us a bit self-conscious.
Usually we are laughing during our evening meal.

Anne gets ready to give her verdict on a recipe I'm testing on some winter dinner guests.

Even in the snow, the Chanticleer is special.

Stocks and Sauces

Chicken Stock

Makes 3 Quarts

5 pounds chicken parts (necks, wings, backs)
3 carrots, peeled and sliced
2 onions, sliced
3 stalks celery, sliced
2 leeks (white part only), sliced
1 clove garlic, crushed
1 large bouquet garni (tie together 2 bay leaves, 3 sprigs thyme, 6 parsley stalks)
2 cloves
6 peppercorns

1. Place the chicken parts in a pot. Cover with cold water and bring to a boil. Skim off the scum that rises to the top. Boil for 5 minutes. Add all the rest of the ingredients. Reduce the heat and simmer for 2 hours.
2. Strain stock through a fine strainer or sieve. Set stock in the refrigerator overnight, then discard the fat that has risen to the top.
3. You can always put the stock back on the fire and let it reduce if you want a more concentrated flavor.

Demi-Glace

Makes about 1 quart

10 pound veal bones (preferably knuckles), cracked into small pieces
6 carrots, sliced
2 onions, sliced
3 stalks celery, sliced
1 head garlic, cut in half but not peeled
3 leeks (white part only), split and thoroughly washed
2 tomatoes, cut in half
1 bouquet garni (bay leaf, thyme, parsley)
12 peppercorns
3 cloves
2 tablespoons tomato paste

1. Place the bones in a roasting pan. Roast in the oven at 450 degrees until the bones start to brown. Add all the vegetables except the leeks and the tomatoes. Put pan back in the oven until the vegetables start to brown.
2. Place the bones and vegetables in a large kettle. Cover with water (at least 1½ gallons). Bring to a boil and carefully skim the top. Simmer for 15 minutes. Add all the remaining ingredients and simmer slowly for 4 hours. Skim the top from time to time, but do not stir the stock as it will get cloudy.
3. Strain the stock first through a colander, then through a fine sieve. Chill overnight and remove the congealed fat.
4. Return the stock to the heat. Bring to a boil and then simmer for an hour or so. Keep on skimming to remove as many impurities as possible. Reduce the stock until it reaches the consistency of heavy cream.

You can freeze this demi-glace in an ice-cube tray, so you can pop one out whenever you need it. If you reduce this demi-glace further, you will have *glace de viande,* the highest concentration possible.

Substitution for demi-glace
Makes about 1 cup

1 twelve-ounce can beef broth
1 twelve-ounce can chicken broth
1 carrot, sliced
1 onion, sliced
1 bouquet garni
1 teaspoon unsalted butter
1 teaspoon flour

Sauté the vegetables in butter until they start getting brown. Add the flour. Stir for a minute. Add both cans of broth and the bouquet garni. Cook for 20 minutes, then strain.

Court Bouillon

Makes 2 quarts

2 quarts water
1 carrot, sliced
1 onion, sliced
1 stalk celery, sliced
1 small bouquet garni (include 2 sprigs of dill)
8 peppercorns
1 cup dry white wine
1 lemon, cut in half
1 tablespoon salt

1. Put all the ingredients in a large pot. Bring to a boil, then cook at slow heat for half an hour, or until vegetables are cooked. Strain.

Court bouillon will keep in the refrigerator for a couple of weeks. Use it as needed for poaching fish, shellfish, sweetbreads, calves brains, etc.

Fish Stock

Makes 1 quart

3 pounds fish racks or heads (use flat fish, cod, or bass; do not use oily fish)
1 tablespoon peanut oil
1 onion, sliced
2 carrots, sliced
2 celery stalks, sliced
1 leek (white part only), sliced
2 cups dry white wine
1 quart cold water
1 bouquet garni (6 sprigs parsley, 2 sprigs thyme, 1 bay leaf)

1. Put the oil in a pan or sauteuse. When hot add the fish bones, previously washed and cleaned of all blood. (Blood will make the fish stock bitter; make sure to remove all gills.) Cook the bones for 5 minutes on high heat. Add the vegetables and continue cooking for another 5 minutes. Stir once in a while.
2. Put the contents of the sauteuse in a pot. Add the wine, 1 quart cold water, and the bouquet garni. Cook for 20 minutes.
3. Strain the stock through a colander, putting pressure on the bones and vegetables to extract all the juices. Pour the stock into a pot.
4. Return the stock to low heat and reduce for 10 minutes. Remove any fat that may have formed on the top.

Fish stock can be frozen for a few weeks. If you reduce this stock further, you will have *glace de poisson*.

Fumet de Moules

Mussel Broth

Makes about 3 cups

2 pounds mussels, thoroughly scrubbed and rinsed
1 ounce unsalted butter
1 medium onion, chopped
6 shallots, chopped
1 stalk celery, chopped
1 bottle dry white wine
1 bouquet garni
1 clove garlic, crushed

1. Put the butter in a large kettle. Let it melt, then add the onion, shallots, and celery. Sweat vegetables for a few minutes. Add white wine, the bouquet garni, and garlic. Boil for 5 minutes.
2. Add the scrubbed mussels. Cover the pan and bring to a fast boil until the mussels open. Do not overcook.
3. Strain the broth and reserve the mussels for another recipe. Return the broth to a medium heat and reduce by one third. Strain through a cheesecloth.

Beurre Blanc Nantais

Makes about ½ cup

3 shallots, chopped
2 ounces white wine
1 teaspoon red wine vinegar
2 tablespoons heavy cream (optional)
5 ounces unsalted butter
juice of half a lemon

1. In a small, heavy-bottomed pan (do not use aluminum), place the shallots, wine, and vinegar. Bring to a boil and reduce until almost dry. Add the cream and reduce by half.
2. Lower heat and, using a wire whip, add the butter a small piece at a time. Whisk until the butter disappears. Keep the sauce warm but not too hot.
3. Add salt, pepper, and lemon juice to taste. Strain the sauce before using.

You can omit the heavy cream. There are two schools in Brittany; one uses cream, the other doesn't. I like both preparations.

Sauce Béchamel

Cream Sauce

Makes about 1 quart

3 tablespoons unsalted butter
4 tablespoons flour
3 cups milk, scalded
1 pinch nutmeg

1. Make a roux in a small pan by melting the butter and then adding the flour. Mix well. Cook slowly for a few minutes until the roux becomes lightly golden.
2. Gradually stir in the scalded milk. Stirring vigorously with a whip, cook the sauce until it starts to boil. Reduce the heat. Add salt and pepper to taste, and a pinch of nutmeg. Keep stirring so the sauce doesn't become lumpy. Simmer for 10 minutes, stirring occasionally.
3. If the sauce is lumpy, strain it.

Béchamel "cream sauce" is the base of many sauces. Add cheese to it, and it becomes sauce mornay. Add lobster purée to make sauce cardinal. Béchamel is so versatile!

Hollandaise

Makes about 1 cup

9 ounces unsalted butter (or 8 ounces clarified butter)
4 tablespoons water
1 teaspoon white wine vinegar
1 shallot, chopped
6 white peppercorns, crushed
3 egg yolks
juice of ½ lemon

1. In a small, non-corrosive pan, put together 3 tablespoons water, the vinegar, shallots, and crushed peppercorns. Bring to a boil and reduce by one third.
2. Melt the butter in a small pan at low temperature. Keep warm.
3. Put the vinegar and shallot reduction in a bain-marie. Add 1 tablespoon water and the egg yolks. Whip for 10 minutes; by then the mixture should be fluffy and tripled in volume. The temperature of the bain-marie should not be too high or the eggs will cook.
4. At this point, whip in the warm melted butter, a small amount at a time. Leave the butter residue in the bottom of the pan. Keep whipping and add the lemon juice and salt.
5. Strain the sauce through cheesecloth or a fine strainer.

Hollandaise can be used for many preparations: to thicken sauces, to glaze dishes, and to be served as a complete sauce in itself.

By adding 3 tablespoons of whipped cream to cooled (but not chilled) hollandaise, you get mousseline sauce, which is very good with asparagus, broccoli, etc.

Sauce Digoinaise

Watercress, Shallot, and Chive Mayonnaise

Makes about 1 cup

2 egg yolks
1 teaspoon Dijon mustard
a pinch of salt
2 teaspoons lemon juice
¾ cup peanut oil
¼ bunch watercress, chopped
1 teaspoon chopped chives
2 shallots, chopped
a few drops of Tabasco

1. Put the egg yolks in a bowl. Add the mustard, a pinch of salt, and 1 teaspoon of lemon juice. Mix all the ingredients with a wire whisk. Continue whisking and slowly incorporate the oil, a drop at a time to start and then in a steady stream. (This is the basic recipe for mayonnaise.)
2. Add another teaspoon of lemon juice. Add the watercress, chives, shallots, and a few drops of Tabasco.

Use this sauce with cold or raw meats. It's great with carpaccio.

Cumberland Sauce

Makes about ½ cup

¼ cup red currant jelly
1 orange
1 lemon
2 shallots, chopped
1 teaspoon dry mustard
1 dash Worcestershire sauce
1 tablespoon glace de viande (see page 83)
1 ounce port
1 dash Tabasco sauce

1. Put the red currant jelly into a small sauce pan. Place the pan on a low heat and let the jelly melt slowly.
2. Peel the orange. Discard all of the white pith. Cut the orange peel into very fine julienne and set aside. Extract juice from the orange and add it to the melted jelly.
3. Repeat this process with the lemon.
4. Drop the julienne of orange and lemon peel into boiling water for a minute. Drain the peel and add it to the sauce.
5. Quickly blanch the chopped shallots and add them to the sauce.
6. Bring the sauce to a boil. Add the mustard, Worcestershire sauce, glace de viande, port, and a dash of Tabasco. Let the sauce cook for 3 minutes, stirring occasionally.
7. Cumberland sauce can be made well ahead as it keeps indefinitely in the refrigerator.

You can make this same sauce with wild beach plums. Pick very ripe beach plums. Use your thumb and index finger to squeeze out the pits. Place the pulp in a pan. Bring to a boil and cook for 5 minutes. Mash up the berries and use instead of red currant jelly. If the berries are ripe enough, you will not need to add any sugar to the beach plum Cumberland sauce.

Sauce Poivrade

Makes 2 cups

1½ pounds lamb bones, cut up
1 teaspoon olive oil
1 carrot, finely diced
1 onion, finely diced
1 stalk celery, finely diced
1 bouquet garni
2 cloves garlic, crushed
4 shallots, chopped
4 mushrooms, sliced
2 ounces flour
1 ounce Cognac
2 ounces red wine vinegar
1 bottle red wine
1 teaspoon crushed peppercorn
1 teaspoon glace de viande (see page 83)

1. Using a frying pan, sauté the lamb bones in olive oil until brown on all sides. Add the mirepoix (small dice) of carrots, onion, and celery, the bouquet garni, garlic, shallots, and mushrooms. Sauté for another 5 minutes.
2. Put all the ingredients in a large ovenproof saucepan. Sprinkle with the flour and mix well. Put in the oven at 400 degrees for 10 minutes to cook the flour.
3. Deglaze the frying pan with the Cognac and the vinegar. Pour the deglazing liquid over the lamb bones. Add the red wine and bring to a boil. Flame. Add the crushed peppercorns and cook slowly for 2 hours.
4. Put the sauce through a china cap or strainer. Press on the bones and vegetables to extract all juices. Put the sauce back into a saucepan. Bring to a boil. Add the glace de viande. Season to taste.

Sauce Chivry

White Wine and Herb Sauce

Makes about 2 cups

½ cup white wine
1 teaspoon chopped chervil
1 teaspoon chopped tarragon
1 teaspoon chopped chives
1 tablespoon chopped watercress
2 cups cream sauce (see page 88)
1 tablespoon chopped, blanched spinach (blanch for 2 minutes)
1 teaspoon chopped parsley
2 tablespoons unsalted butter or 2 tablespoons hollandaise (see page 89)

1. Put the wine and all of the herbs, except the parsley and spinach, in a non-corrosive pan. Bring to a boil and reduce to one third. Add the cream sauce and cook at low heat for 3 to 4 minutes.
2. Pour the sauce through a strainer to remove the herbs. Put the sauce in the blender and add the spinach and parsley. When smooth, return to the pan.
3. Add the butter or hollandaise to the sauce. Season with salt and pepper. Keep warm but do not boil.

This sauce will do very well with lobster soufflé, poached fish, or poached poultry.

Sauce Oseille, Ciboulette

Sorrel and Chive Sauce

Makes 1 cup

3½ ounces sorrel leaves
1 tablespoon chopped chives
2 shallots, chopped
½ teaspoon chopped tarragon
1 tablespoon dry white wine
1 cup heavy cream
½ teaspoon lemon juice

1. Wash the sorrel leaves and discard the stems. Put the sorrel in a pot with the chives, shallots, tarragon, white wine, and a spoonful of the cream. Bring to a boil and cook for 2 minutes. Run the mixture in a blender until it is smooth. Set aside and let cool.
2. Whip the remaining cream until it starts to get thick. (Do not let it get too stiff.) Add the purée of herbs, a few drops of lemon juice, salt, and pepper.

Sauce Cressonnette

Watercress Sauce

Makes about ¾ cup

¼ bunch watercress
4 ounces Champagne
2 shallots, chopped
2 tablespoons reduced fish stock (see page 85, or use clam juice)
¾ cup heavy cream
1 teaspoon lemon juice
1 ounce unsalted butter

1. Blanch the watercress in boiling water. Purée the watercress in the blender and set aside.
2. In a saucepan, put the Champagne, the chopped shallots, and the reduced fish stock (glace de poisson). Reduce to one tablespoon. Add the cream and lemon juice. Bring to a boil and reduce until the sauce starts to thicken. Remove from heat and whip in the butter, a small amount at a time. Taste for salt and pepper.
3. Add the purée of watercress to the sauce.

Sauce Mousse de Cresson (ou de Tomates)

Cold Watercress (or Tomato) Mousse Sauce

Makes about 2 cups

1 bunch watercress (for tomato mousse, use 3 tablespoons peeled, seeded, chopped tomatoes
   and 1 tablespoon tomato paste instead of the watercress)
2 teaspoons unsalted butter
1 tablespoon chopped shallots
1 tablespoon chopped tarragon
1 pinch chopped garlic
2 tablespoons dry white wine
11 ounces heavy cream
2 leaves gelatin, soaked in water
1 teaspoon lemon juice

1. Cut the stems and wash the watercress.
2. Put butter in a pan and melt slowly. Add the chopped shallots and cook for a minute,
stirring constantly so they do not brown. Add the watercress (or tomatoes), the chopped
tarragon, chopped garlic, and white wine. Cover and cook for a minute. Add half of the
cream. Salt and pepper to taste. Bring to a boil and reduce for 7 to 10 minutes over
medium heat.
3. Remove from the heat and add the soaked gelatin. Dissolve.
4. Pour the mixture into the blender. Add the lemon juice and blend until smooth.
Refrigerate.
5. Put the remaining cream in a bowl. Whip lightly until it starts to get thick. Add the
thickened cream to the watercress sauce. Mix well and check seasoning.

Sauce aux Tomates et aux Herbes

Cold Tomato and Herb Sauce

Makes about 2 cups

4 vine-ripened tomatoes, peeled and seeded
2 cloves garlic, crushed
2 tablespoons chopped chervil
2 tablespoons chopped parsley
2 tablespoons chopped tarragon
1 teaspoon chopped dill
1 shallot, finely chopped
10 coriander seeds, crushed
3 tablespoons olive oil
½ teaspoon freshly grated orange peel

1. Chop the peeled, seeded tomatoes very finely.
2. Place all the ingredients in a saucepan. Cover and stew at low heat for half an hour. Add salt and pepper to taste.
3. Refrigerate the sauce.

This sauce may be served with many cold fish dishes and with fish terrines.

Fondue de Tomates

Tomato Fondue

Makes about 2 cups

2 pounds ripe tomatoes
1 teaspoon olive oil
2 cloves garlic, crushed
1 bouquet garni

1. Peel and seed the tomatoes. (Drop them in boiling water for a minute, remove the skins, cut them in half, and squeeze to remove the seeds.) Chop the tomatoes coarsely.
2. Put the olive oil in a pot. When hot, add the chopped tomatoes, the crushed garlic, and the bouquet garni. Cook over low heat for 30 minutes.
3. Remove garlic and bouquet garni. Add salt and pepper to taste.

The tomato fondue can be made ahead and stored in the refrigerator.

Soups

Gratinée Normande

Onion Soup, Normandy Style

Serves 4

3 to 4 medium Bermuda onions
2 tablespoons unsalted butter
1 bouquet garni
1 cup plus 4 tablespoons hard apple cider
2 teaspoons flour
3 cups chicken stock (see page 82)
1 pinch nutmeg
⅓ cup heavy cream
8 thin slices French bread
2 tablespoons grated Swiss cheese

1. Peel the onions and slice them very thinly. Put a tablespoon of butter in a sauteuse. Add the sliced onion and sauté until the onion starts to get light brown. Add the bouquet garni and 1 cup of cider. Cook for 5 minutes, then set aside.
2. In a saucepan, make a roux with the remaining tablespoon of butter and the flour. Add the chicken stock. Stirring with a whip, bring the thickened stock to the boil. Simmer for 15 minutes.
3. Add the onions to the chicken velouté. Cook slowly for 15 minutes. Season with salt, pepper, and a pinch of nutmeg. Add cream. Keep warm but do not boil.
4. Divide the remaining cider among 4 ovenproof soup bowls. Pour in the onion soup. Place the slices of bread on top. Sprinkle with grated cheese.
5. Place soup under broiler until golden brown.

Much lighter than the old classic. The Bermuda onions add a different dimension. Make sure to use a good cider, not too sweet.

Wine notes
Any dry white wine will be good, but I would probably drink an Alsatian wine, maybe a spicy Gewurztraminer.

Gazpacho Andalou

Serves 6

6 ripe tomatoes, peeled
2 green peppers, seeded
2 red peppers, seeded
4 cucumbers, peeled
1 clove garlic, crushed
2 boiled eggs (yolks only)
1 teaspoon olive oil
1 pinch dry mustard
1 pinch cumin
1 teaspoon red wine vinegar
1 teaspoon chopped chervil
1 teaspoon chopped shallots
6 slices lemon (for garnish)
1 cucumber, peeled, seeded, and diced (for garnish)

1. Cut the peeled tomatoes in half and squeeze out the seeds. Cut the peppers in half and discard the seeds. Cut the peeled cucumber in half lengthways and scoop out the seeds.
2. Put all the vegetables and the garlic in the blender and run until smooth.
3. Take the yolks from the hard-boiled eggs and put them in a bowl. Mix them with the olive oil to make a paste. Add the mustard and cumin. Mix well. Add the paste to the vegetable purée. Add vinegar, chopped shallots, chopped chervil, and salt and pepper to taste. Blend well.
4. Keep ice cold until serving.
5. Serve in cold bowls. Garnish with diced cucumber and a slice of lemon.

This is the real thing. A Spanish friend made it for me. He used hot peppers. It was great.

Soupe aux Concombres et Tomates

Cucumber and Tomato Soup

Serves 6

1 cucumber (seedless European type), peeled
6 medium tomatoes, peeled, seeded, and chopped
1 tablespoon olive oil
1 onion, chopped
1 clove garlic, chopped
1 quart chicken stock (see page 82)
2 sprigs dill
1 tablespoon sugar
1 pinch nutmeg
3 tablespoons sour cream
1 tablespoon chopped parsley

1. Peel the cucumber. Cut part of the cucumber into small dices (to make 2 tablespoons). Set aside. Cut the rest of the cucumber into slices.
2. Put the oil in a large saucepan. When hot, add the onion, tomatoes, and garlic. Stew for 5 minutes. Pour the chicken stock over the vegetables. Add the dill, sugar, nutmeg, and sliced cucumbers. Bring to a boil, then simmer for 30 minutes.
3. Put the soup in the blender. Run until smooth.
4. Chill the soup. When cold, whip in the sour cream. Add the previously diced cucumbers and salt and pepper to taste. Serve in cold bowls. Sprinkle with chopped parsley.

Very summery, very cool. Use nice, vine-ripened tomatoes.

Crème de Ciboulette

Cream of Chives Soup

Serves 6

½ cup chopped chives
4 leeks (white part only)
1 medium onion, sliced
12 leaves sorrel, shredded (if available)
2 large potatoes, peeled and sliced
3 cups chicken stock
1 cup milk
½ cup heavy cream
1 pinch nutmeg
lemon juice (to taste)
1 teaspoon chopped chervil (if you can get it)

1. Thoroughly wash the leeks and slice them.
2. Melt a little butter in a heavy pot. Add the leeks, onions, and sorrel. Cook slowly for 5 minutes. Do not brown. Add the sliced potato, chicken stock, milk, salt, and pepper. Cook for 30 to 40 minutes. Remove from heat and add the chopped chives.
3. When the soup has cooled down, put it in the blender. Run until smooth. Add the cream, a scraping of nutmeg, and a few drops of lemon juice. Taste for seasoning.
4. Serve in cold bowls. Sprinkle with chopped chervil.

This is a variation of the old standby, so much abused vichyssoise. The sorrel and chives give it a new taste and a little excitement.

Crème d'Artichauts

Cold Artichoke Soup

Serves 6

6 artichokes
1 quart chicken stock (see page 82)
¼ cup heavy cream
1 pinch sugar
1 pinch nutmeg
2 teaspoons chopped herbs (parsley, chives, chervil)

1. Cook the artichokes in salted, boiling water until the leaves detach easily from the heart (about 30 minutes). Run under cold water. Peel off leaves and remove the chokes.
2. Cut up the artichoke bottoms and put them in a pot with the chicken stock. Bring to a boil and then simmer for 10 minutes. Run artichoke bottoms and chicken stock in the blender until smooth. Let soup cool off.
3. In a bowl, whip the cream until it starts to thicken. Mix it into the chilled artichoke soup. Add salt, pepper, sugar, nutmeg, and herbs. Serve in chilled bowls.

You can also serve this soup hot; just don't whip the heavy cream before you add it (step 3).

Soupe de Grenouilles

Frog Leg Soup

Serves 6

18 frog legs (small if possible)
1 bottle dry white wine
1 carrot, sliced
1 carrot, cut into julienne
1 onion, sliced
1 stalk celery, sliced
1 stalk celery, cut into julienne
1 leek (white part only), cut into julienne
1 bouquet garni
8 peppercorns
2 cloves
4 cloves garlic, crushed
2 tablespoons unsalted butter
2 tablespoons flour
2 egg yolks
½ cup heavy cream
juice of ½ lemon
2 teaspoons chopped parsley

1. Make a court bouillon in a large pot by combining 1 quart water, the white wine, the sliced carrot, sliced celery, sliced onion, bouquet garni, peppercorns, cloves, and crushed garlic. Cook for 20 minutes.

2. Cook the julienned vegetables (carrot, leeks, celery) in boiling salted water for 3 minutes. Run under cold water to stop cooking. Drain and set aside.

3. Poach the frog legs in the court bouillon until the meat pulls easily off the bone (about 6 to 8 minutes). Remove the frog legs from the broth and set aside to cool.

4. Strain the broth and keep warm. In a small pan, make a roux by melting the butter; when melted and frothing, add the flour. Stir with a whip. Cook for 2 to 3 minutes; do not brown. Add this roux to the broth. Whip vigorously to avoid lumps. Bring to a boil, then simmer for 10 minutes, stirring occasionally.

5. Remove all bones from frog legs.

6. In a small bowl, put the yolks, the cream, and the juice of ½ lemon. Whip together. Add this mixture (the liaison) to the soup. Do not boil. Stir and add salt and pepper to taste.

7. To the now finished soup, add the boned frog legs and the vegetable julienne. Let everything warm up for a minute. Serve with chopped parsley sprinkled on top.

A long recipe, but not terribly complicated. A nice way to start a dinner, or have it for lunch. The soup is almost a light stew.

Wine notes
A dry Riesling would be appropriate with this soup.

Soupe de Poisson en Croûte

Shellfish Stew in Puff Pastry

Serves 6

12 raw oysters, freshly shucked
24 mussels, scrubbed, rinsed, and steamed in their own juices
8 ounces of scallops
2 teaspoons unsalted butter
2 teaspoons flour
1 quart fish stock (see page 85, or substitute a can of clam juice)
1 pinch saffron
¼ cup heavy cream
1 leek (white part only), cut into julienne
1 carrot, cut into julienne
1 pound puff pastry (frozen is fine)
1 egg

1. Make a roux by melting butter and adding flour. Mix with a whip and cook for 2 to 3 minutes.
2. Add the roux to the fish stock. Bring to a boil, stirring constantly. This velouté should reach the consistency of heavy cream.
3. Add the saffron to the velouté and cook for a few minutes. Add the cream and continue cooking for 5 more minutes. Also, taste for salt and pepper.
4. In the bottom of each ovenproof soup bowl, place 2 oysters, 4 mussels, some scallops, and some of the leek and carrot julienne. Cover with the velouté to within ¼ inch of the top of each bowl. Be careful not to overfill the bowls, as the mixture will seep out during baking.
5. Cut 6 tops out of the puff pastry. Make sure to cut them wide enough to overlap comfortably the sides of the bowl. (Unless you want to make your own, you can buy very good frozen puff pastry in your local grocery store.)
6. Brush the outer rim of each bowl with egg wash and cover each bowl with a pastry top. Press pastry tightly against the sides of the bowl.
7. Brush each puff pastry top with egg wash and make a small slit in the center so that the steam can escape. Bake at 350 degrees for 10 minutes.

Wine notes
For a good winter lunch, serve with a bottle of Sauvignon Blanc from California – crisp, and a lot of fruit.

Crème de Homard

Cream of Lobster Soup

Serves 6

1 two-pound lobster, live
2 ounces unsalted butter
1 carrot, diced
1 onion, diced
1 leek (white part only), sliced
1 stalk celery, diced
1 ounce Cognac
1 cup dry white wine
½ gallon water or fish stock (see page 85)
1 clove garlic, crushed
1 small tomato, crushed
1 pinch saffron
1 pinch cayenne pepper
1 bouquet garni
¼ cup heavy cream

1. Cut the lobster in half. Remove the meat and set it aside. Chop the head and carapace with a heavy knife. Chop the shell into very small pieces so that it won't strain your blender later.
2. In a heavy kettle or pot, melt half of the butter and then add the diced carrot, onion, leek, celery, and the chopped-up lobster shell. Sauté until the shell starts to turn red. Flame with the Cognac. Add the white wine, half a gallon of water (I prefer to use fish stock), the garlic, the crushed tomato, the saffron, the cayenne, and the bouquet garni. Bring to a boil and simmer for 30 minutes.
3. Dice the lobster meat and reserve one third of it.
4. Put the other two thirds of the lobster meat in the already cooked bisque and cook for another 5 minutes. Let the bisque cool down before proceeding with the next step.
5. Put the bisque in a blender until all the ingredients are thoroughly puréed. Strain bisque through a fine sieve, pour into a clean pot, and return to heat. Stirring constantly, bring the bisque to a boil and add the remaining lobster meat. Cook for 3 to 4 minutes. Remove from the heat and add the remaining butter and the cream. Taste for salt and pepper.

A rather elaborate and expensive soup, but what a delight and also very festive for the holidays.

Wine notes
I like to serve a glass of Sauternes with this dish. What an experience!

Crème d'Huîtres

Cream of Oyster Soup

Serves 4

2 dozen oysters (if fresh not available, use frozen)
2 stalks celery, finely diced
1 onion, finely diced
4 scallions, finely sliced
4 tablespoons unsalted butter
3 tablespoons flour
2 quarts fish stock (see page 85, or use clam juice)
1 clove garlic, finely chopped
1 pinch saffron
½ pint heavy cream
4 ounces dry sherry

1. Open oysters and save the juice.
2. Poach the oysters in their own juice for 3 minutes. Make sure they do not boil. Set aside.
3. In a soup kettle, melt 3 tablespoons of butter and lightly sauté the diced celery and onions until tender. Keep the heat low so that the vegetables do not brown. Sprinkle with 3 tablespoons of flour. Cook slowly for 5 minutes, stirring occasionally with a wooden spoon.
4. Add 2 quarts fish stock (or clam juice), the liquid from the oysters, the chopped garlic clove, the sliced scallions, and a pinch of saffron. Bring to a fast boil, sitrring constantly. Lower heat and simmer for 20 minutes.
5. Add the cream and the sherry. Correct the seasoning with freshly ground pepper and the remaining butter. Add the oysters and continue cooking for 2 minutes. Do not boil. Serve with oyster crackers or croutons.

This soup is just like velvet, especially on a cold, windy day. Make plenty of it because there is never enough. A nice, fresh baguette only adds to the pleasure.

Wine notes
A crisp white wine like a Chablis will make for a great combination.

Crème de Moules Glacée

Cold Cream of Mussel Soup with Curry and Cucumbers

Serves 8

2 pounds mussels, thoroughly scrubbed and rinsed
1 cup dry white wine
1 teaspoon olive oil
1 onion, chopped
2 leeks (white part only), sliced
2 cloves garlic, crushed
1 pound tomatoes, peeled, seeded, and chopped
2 medium cucumbers, peeled, seeded, and sliced
1 quart fish stock (see page 85)
1 pinch saffron
1 teaspoon curry powder
1 bouquet garni
1 pinch cayenne pepper
¾ cup heavy cream
1 teaspoon chopped chives
½ cup chopped cucumbers (for garnish)

1. Pour the white wine in a non-corrosive pan. Add the previously scrubbed and washed mussels. Cover and bring to a boil. Stirring occasionally, cook until the mussels open up. Remove the mussels from the shell and set aside. Filter the broth through a cheesecloth. Set aside.
2. Put the olive oil in a heavy pot. When warm, add the chopped onions and the sliced leeks. Stir for a couple of minutes, making sure that the vegetables don't get brown. Add the crushed garlic and the chopped-up tomatoes. Cook for a few minutes. Add the sliced cucumbers. Pour in the fish stock and strained mussel broth. Add the saffron, curry powder, bouquet garni, and cayenne pepper. Simmer until the vegetables are soft.
3. Let the soup cool and then put it in the blender. Run until smooth. Mix in the cream and chives.
4. Serve the soup in chilled bowls. Garnish each bowl with a tablespoon of chopped cucumber and a few steamed mussels.

A very successful combination and not too hot – but if hot food is a must, by all means increase the curry powder to a tablespoon.

Wine notes
I may be partial, but I would drink Muscadet with this soup.

Appetizers

Coquillages au Champagne

Shellfish Stewed in Champagne

Serves 6

12 oysters, shucked
¼ cup steamed mussels
¼ cup cooked periwinkles (see note below)
1 cup Champagne
2 tablespoons heavy cream
3 ounces unsalted butter
1 leek (white part only), cut into julienne and lightly blanched
1 carrot, cut into julienne and lightly blanched

1. Bring the Champagne to a boil. Drop in the oysters and cook for two minutes. Remove the oysters and set aside.
2. Drop in the mussels and periwinkles. Let them warm up for a minute, then remove and set aside.
3. Bring the Champagne to a boil again. Add the cream and reduce by half. Remove from heat and quickly whisk in the butter, a small amount at a time. Check the seasoning. Add the shellfish.
4. Serve on a warm plate. Garnish with a sprinkle of lightly blanched leek and carrot julienne.

Periwinkles are small sea snails, not easily available at any fish market but worth trying to get. Here on Nantucket, I just go to the beach and get them.

This dish is delicious even without periwinkles, but they do add an exotic flavor that is unlike any other kind of shellfish. You can substitute littleneck clams for the periwinkles, but be sure not to overcook them.

Should you be able to buy fresh periwinkles, here is what to do with them: wash them under running water and then cook them for 3 to 4 minutes in salted boiling water. Also add the juice of half a lemon to the water. Drain the periwinkles and let them cool. Pick the meat out of the shells.

Wine notes
Why not serve Champagne?

Huîtres au Caviar

Oysters Stewed in Mussel Broth with Caviar

Serves 4

24 oysters
2 cups mussel broth (see page 86)
2 ounces unsalted butter
4 ounces caviar (I like to use Palaid sturgeon caviar from the East Coast.
  It has less salt than the West Coast caviar.)

1. Boil the mussel broth until it is reduced by one third. Keep warm.
2. Open the oysters and cut them loose from the shell. Drain them on a towel. Then arrange them on four small, deep plates.
3. Whip the butter (a small amount at a time) into the hot mussel broth. Pour the broth over the oysters but do not cover (about half way).
4. Put the plates with the oysters and broth under the salamander or broiler for about 2 minutes at medium heat.
5. Sprinkle the caviar over the oysters. Serve this dish right away, since the caviar has a tendency to turn grey under heat.

I use strictly Nantucket farmed oysters. They are, in my mind, one of the best oysters you can find – very salty and clean. They remind me of the wild oysters we get in Brittany.

Wine notes
This is a rich appetizer. I would serve one of those big, luscious California Chardonnays or a Chassagne-Montrachet.

Flan de Moules au Coulis de Cresson

Mussel Custard with Watercress Coulis

Serves 6

2 pounds mussels, thoroughly scrubbed and rinsed
4 tablespoons unsalted butter
2 shallots, finely chopped
1 tablespoon finely chopped parsley
¼ cup dry white wine
1 sprig thyme
1 pinch finely chopped garlic
1 pint heavy cream
4 eggs
1 pinch saffron
1 pinch nutmeg
1 bunch watercress

1. Melt 3½ tablespoons butter in a large kettle. Add the shallots and the parsley, and stir for 2 minutes over medium heat. Add the cleaned mussels, white wine, thyme, and garlic. Cook for about 5 to 7 minutes (just until mussels open). Take the mussels out of their shells. Strain the broth through a cheese cloth and save it.
2. In a mixing bowl, whip together 10 ounces of cream, 4 eggs, half of the mussel broth, saffron, nutmeg, salt, and freshly ground pepper to taste. When all the ingredients are thoroughly blended, carefully mix in the mussels using a wooden spoon in order not to break them.
3. Butter 6 small ramekins and fill them with the mixture. Set the ramekins in a shallow pan of water (a bain-marie) and cook for 8 to 12 minutes in a medium oven (325 degrees).
4. Unmold each flan onto a plate. Serve with a watercress coulis on the side.

Watercress Coulis
1. Wash the watercress and cut 2 inches off the stems. Cook the watercress in boiling, salted water just until the stems become tender. Run it under cold water and drain.
2. Purée the watercress with a tablespoon of mussel broth in a blender. Add 6 ounces of heavy cream and blend for 1 minute more. Pour mixture into a saucepan and bring to a quick boil. Remove from heat and whip in ½ tablespoon of butter to thicken.

Wine notes
I would serve a Chardonnay on the austere side or a Grand Cru Chablis.

Mousse de St. Jacques
au Beurre Blanc Nantais

Scallop Mousse with Beurre Blanc Sauce

Serves 4

16 ounces scallops (if possible, use bay scallops)
3 eggs
5 egg yolks
2 cups milk, boiled and cooled
2 cups heavy cream
1 pinch nutmeg

1. Grind the scallops and then force them through a fine sieve. Put them in a bowl and add the eggs, yolks, cold boiled milk, cream, nutmeg, and salt and white pepper to taste. Mix the ingredients together with a whip. Pass mixture once more through a fine sieve.
2. Butter four small ramekins and fill them with the mousse. Cover with foil and poach in a bain-marie for 15 to 20 minutes at 300 to 350 degrees.
3. Unmold the mousse onto a plate and pour beurre blanc nantais around it (see page 87).

Elegant simplicity with my favorite sauce, beurre blanc, which originated in Nantes, my hometown in Brittany. Beurre blanc was served with brochet, the pike from the Loire river. On Sundays all the little auberges and bistrots along the river serve *brochet au beurre blanc*, and they each have their own authentic version of the sauce.

Wine notes
A Pouilly-Fumé sounds perfect to me.

Terrine de Saumon et de St. Jacques

Salmon and Scallop Mousse

Serves 12

10½ ounces scallops
10½ ounces sole filets
14 ounces salmon filets
2 cups heavy cream
4 egg yolks
2 pinches of nutmeg
2 pinches of cayenne pepper
4 ounces Armagnac
8 egg whites
2 tablespoons lemon juice
1 medium seedless European cucumber, peeled
1 teaspoon chopped dill

1. Make a forcemeat by putting the scallops and the sole in the food processor. Run until smooth. Put the mixture in a bowl. Add 1 cup cream, 2 egg yolks, salt, white pepper, a pinch nutmeg, a pinch cayenne, and 2 ounces Armagnac. Mix well. Add 4 egg whites, one at a time. Keep on mixing. Add 1 tablespoon of lemon juice.
2. Put this forcemeat through a fine sieve. Set aside in the refrigerator.
3. Make a forcemeat with the salmon, using the same method and the same ingredients as above. Set aside in refrigerator.
4. Cut the peeled cucumber lengthwise into ¼ inch thick slices. Slice the cucumber again into sticks ¼ inch thick. (Each stick should be the length of the cucumber.)
5. Butter a terrine mold and line it with parchment paper. Place a layer of salmon forcemeat in the bottom. Arrange a layer of cucumber sticks on top. Now put on a layer of scallop forcemeat and another layer of cucumber sticks. Repeat these procedures until all the forcemeats have been used up.
6. Cover the terrine with foil and place it in a bain-marie. Cook at 350 degrees for 40 to 50 minutes. Let the terrine rest in the refrigerator overnight before serving.
7. Serve with a watercress mousse sauce (see page 95) and with a tomato mousse sauce (see page 95). Cover half of a cold plate with watercress mousse sauce, the other half with tomato mousse sauce. Place a slice of the terrine on top of the sauces. You can also serve the terrine with just one sauce.

When you add cream to any preparation done in a blender or food processor, make sure you mix in the cream by hand; if you mix it by machine, the cream will turn to butter.

Wine notes
A four or five year old Meursault will be a good balance to this terrine, which has a slight acidity to it because of the lemon and tomato. A California Chardonnay will also be very good; keep it on the soft side and not too oaky.

Pâté d'Anguille

Eel Pâté in Pastry Crust

2 pounds eel filets (if unavailable, use salmon)
1 pound sole filets
1 cup dry white wine
¼ cup olive oil
1 teaspoon chopped parsley
1 teaspoon chopped tarragon
1 teaspoon chopped basil
1 teaspoon chopped chervil
4 egg whites (reserve 1 for brushing pastry)
½ cup heavy cream
1 pinch nutmeg
1 twelve inch crêpe (see page 193)
1 pound pâte brisée (see page 223)
1 cup fish aspic (see below)

1. Cut the eel filets lengthwise into thin slices. Marinate for a few hours in white wine, olive oil, the chopped herbs, and salt and pepper to taste.
2. Make a forcemeat by grinding up the sole and by then adding the egg whites, cream, salt, pepper, and a pinch of nutmeg.
3. Remove the eel filets from the marinade. Dry off on a towel.
4. In the center of the crêpe, alternate layers of forcement with layers of eels. Finish off with forcemeat on the top. Wrap the crêpe tightly over the fish.
5. Roll out the pastry and paint the entire surface with egg white. Wrap the pastry around the pâté. Seal both ends with egg white, then paint the entire pâté with egg white.
6. Cover with foil and bake slowly at 350 degrees for 1 hour 15 minutes.
7. When cooked, make a small hole in the top of the pâté and pour the cool aspic inside. Use a teaspoon, baster, or small funnel for this procedure. (You may have to do this 6 or 8 times.) Make sure the aspic does not get too cold or it will solidify.
8. Serve with a cold tomato and herb sauce (see page 96).

Fish Aspic
1 cup fish stock (or canned clam juice)
4 leaves or 1 tablespoon gelatin

Bring fish stock to a boil. Add the presoaked gelatin. Let aspic cool.

Wine notes
A crisp Sauvignon Blanc with some substance, not too light.

Fricassée d'Escargots

Stewed Snails with Hazelnuts

Serves 4

24 snails (canned)
16 whole hazelnuts
1 pinch nutmeg
1 teaspoon olive oil
2 shallots, chopped
8 medium mushrooms, diced
3 ounces Cognac
6 ounces red wine
1 clove garlic, chopped
1 tablespoon chopped parsley
1 teaspoon chopped tarragon
1 tablespoon glace de viande (see page 83)
4 ounces unsalted butter

1. Place the hazelnuts on a sheet pan. Roast them in the oven at 450 degrees until light brown. Rub the toasted nuts in a towel to remove the skins. Chop the hazelnuts coarsely.
2. Rinse the (canned) escargots under cold water. Dry them in a towel. Salt and pepper them, and add a touch of nutmeg.
3. Place a medium sized sauteuse on the fire. Add a teaspoon of olive oil and the chopped shallots. Sweat for a minute or two. Add the mushrooms. Sauté them until all the liquid has evaporated. Add the escargots and the chopped hazelnuts. Flame with Cognac. Add the red wine, garlic, and chopped herbs. Bring to a boil and remove the escargots. Keep them warm.
4. Reduce the sauce by one third. Add the glace de viande. Whip in the butter a small amount at a time. Taste for seasoning and add a little freshly ground pepper. Put the escargots back in the sauce. Do not boil at this point.
5. Serve in puff pastry shells or on warm plates garnished with fried croutons. Sprinkle on top with chopped chervil.

For a great lunch, serve the escargots on a bed of fresh pasta. Just plan on 8 to 12 snails per person for a main course.

Wine notes
A sturdy Côte de Beaune will match this dish well.

Mousse de Canard Fondante

Duck Mousse with Armagnac

Serves 8

1 four-pound duck
11 ounces duck liver
6½ ounces unsalted fatback
2 teaspoons salt
½ teaspoon pepper
1 tablespoon peanut oil
1 pinch *quatre épices* (available at a gourmet shop, or make your own by mixing together 125 grams white pepper, 10 grams ground cloves, 30 grams ground ginger, and 35 grams ground nutmeg.)
1 cup heavy cream
4 egg yolks
1 ounce Armagnac
2 ounces raisins, soaked in warm water

1. Remove the legs from the duck. (Save them for confit or cuisse de canard farci.) Place the duck in a roasting pan. Rub with half the salt and pepper. Brush with oil. Roast at 400 degrees for 30 to 40 minutes. The meat must remain pink. When cooked, set aside.
2. Put the fatback in the bowl of a food processor and run until smooth. Add the livers, the remaining salt and pepper, and the pinch of *quatre épices*. Run processor until the texture is smooth. Pour the cream, egg yolks, and Armagnac over the mixture and run for another 30 seconds.
3. Put this mixture through a fine sieve into a mixing bowl. Add the raisins (previously soaked in warm water).
4. Remove the breasts from the roasted duck and discard the skin. Dice the meat into ¼ inch cubes. Mix the diced duck meat into the liver mixture.
5. Pour the forcemeat into a shallow baking dish (3 inches high maximum). Cover with foil and place in a bain-marie. Bake at 350 degrees for 30 minutes.
6. Refrigerate over night.
7. Use two spoons to mold the terrine into the shape of quenelles. Serve with a Cumberland sauce (see page 91) and toasted French bread slices.

This mousse is the epitome of what a mousse should be. It is so good you will want to have it on your toast for breakfast. (I am serious.) Make sure that you keep the breasts cooked pink. You had better undercook them so the colour of the mousse will be a light pink. Shape the mousse with two spoons into the shape of a football. Serve some thin slices of toasted French bread with it.

Wine notes
A glass of Sauternes with the mousse would be a great marriage. I would have a younger Sauternes, maybe 4 or 5 years old.

Salade Nouvelle

Duck Liver and Spinach Salad

Serves 4

1 pound large, fresh duck livers (if desperate, you can use chicken livers)
1 cup chicken stock (see page 82)
1 package fresh spinach
2 hard-boiled eggs, yolks only
2 teaspoons Dijon mustard
juice of half a lemon
⅝ cup olive oil
1 teaspoon peanut oil
1 tablespoon red wine vinegar

1. Clean and rinse the duck livers.
2. Bring the chicken stock to a boil. Plunge the livers into the boiling stock for 1 minute. Take the livers out of the stock and refrigerate.
3. Meanwhile, prepare the spinach salad. Thoroughly wash and dry the spinach. Mash the hard-boiled egg yolks with the mustard, lemon juice, and salt and pepper to taste. Slowly stir in the olive oil. Toss the spinach in the dressing.
4. Cut the cold livers into thin slices. Season with salt and pepper. Brown the liver slices in hot peanut oil for 10 seconds on each side.
5. Arrange the livers on the bed of spinach.
6. Pour off the oil remaining in the pan and add the vinegar. Pour a few drops of the deglazing vinegar on top of each slice of liver.

A nice way to start a meal, this salad will stimulate your appetite. Keep the livers underdone when you sauté them.

Wine notes
A glass of old sherry (at least 20 years old) is a great match with the salade nouvelle. An old Madeira (Bual) is not bad either.

Foie Gras aux Raisins

Sautéed Fat Duck Livers with Sauternes and Grapes

Serves 6

18 ounces fresh foie gras
1 pound white, seedless grapes
1 teaspoon sugar
1 ouhce red wine vinegar
¼ cup Sauternes
¼ cup duck stock or *glace de canard* (duck stock reduced until it is the consistency of
   heavy cream)

1. A fresh foie gras is recommended for this recipe. If you can't get fresh, use *au naturel*.
Do not use a cooked foie gras as you cannot sauté it.
2. Slice the liver into fairly thick scaloppini. Sauté in a heavy skillet. Do not use any fat in
the skillet. Cook for 2 minutes on each side. Remove from pan and keep warm between
two plates.
3. Discard the fat left in the pan. Add the grapes and the sugar. Cook until the grapes start
to caramelize. Deglaze with vinegar. Reduce and add the Sauternes. Reduce and add the
duck stock or, preferably, glace de canard. Reduce again.
4. Arrange the warm slices of sautéed liver on individual plates. Pour the sauce over the
liver. Serve immediately.

You can get very good, fresh, duck foie gras from New York State at a pretty good price.
Check with your butcher or specialty food store.

Wine notes
Sauternes, of course.

Flan de Foie de Canard á l'Aigre Doux

Duck Liver Custard with a Sweet and Sour Sauce

Serves 6

5 large duck livers
½ cup and 2 tablespoons milk
1 teaspoon Armagnac
1 tablespoon unsalted butter
1½ cup demi-glace (see page 83)
1 clove garlic, crushed
1 pinch nutmeg
1 egg yolk
3 eggs
1 cup heavy cream
1 cup red wine vinegar
3½ tablespooons granulated sugar
3 dozen white seedless grapes

1. Clean the duck livers and soak them in ½ cup milk for 4 hours.
2. Drain the livers and rinse them under cold water. Marinate the livers for 2 hours in Armagnac, salt and pepper to taste.
3. Butter 6 four-ounce ramekins. Set in a bain-marie (shallow pan of water).
4. Put the livers in the blender. Add 1 tablespoon of demi-glace, the garlic, nutmeg, and salt and pepper to taste. Blend until smooth. Strain the mixture to make sure that there are no stringy parts left.
5. Put the mixture in a bowl. Mix in the egg yolk, the eggs, 2 tablespoons of the milk, and ½ cup of the cream. Add salt and pepper if needed.
6. Pour the mixture into the ramekins. Place ramekins in a bain-marie and bake for 20 minutes in the oven at 350 degrees.
7. Put the vinegar and sugar in a heavy sauce pan. Cook it to a light caramel stage. Add the rest of the demi-glace. Bring to a boil and reduce for a few minutes. Add ½ cup of cream and boil for about 5 minutes. Add salt, pepper, and a sprinkle of vinegar if needed. The sauce should be acidic.
8. Take the flan out of the ramekins by flipping them upside down. Pour the sauce around each flan. Garnish with fresh white grapes sautéed in unsalted butter.

A very simple, fast appetizer from Les Landes district in southwest France. I spent almost a year in Mont-de-Marsan and learned to love the food in that part of France – the confits and foies gras, the serious earthy cooking down there.

   Make sure you use the lightest coloured livers for this recipe. If duck livers are not available, use chicken livers. Don't overcook the custards.

Wine notes
With the acidity of this dish, I would have a young light red wine from the Southwest – Cahors, perhaps, or Côte de Buzet.

Terrine de Lapin

Rabbit Pâté

Serves 12

7 ounces boned rabbit meat
17 ounces pork
3 ounces dark rum
3 ounces red wine
1 carrot, coarsely chopped
3 shallots, coarsely chopped
2 stalks celery, coarsely chopped
2 sprigs thyme
1 sprig rosemary
2 bay leaves
2 sprigs tarragon
½ bunch parsley
2 eggs
3½ ounces whole, shelled hazelnuts
3½ ounces unsalted fatback (or use sliced bacon)

1. In a bowl, put the rabbit, pork, rum, wine, carrot, shallots, celery, thyme, rosemary, bay leaves, tarragon, parsley, salt and pepper to taste.
2. Marinate for 2 days.
3. Discard the herbs from the marinade and put everything else from the bowl into the food processor. Be sure to keep the mixture coarse. Put the ground-up mixture in a bowl and blend in the eggs and the hazelnuts. Taste for seasoning.
4. Line a pâté mold with thin slices of the fatback or bacon. Fill with the forcemeat. Place the mold in a bain-marie and bake for 1 hour at 325 degrees.
5. Press the pâté by placing a heavy plate or board over it. Put the pâté in the refrigerator for a day before taking it out of the mold.
6. Serve with a Cumberland sauce made with wild beach plums (see page 91).

What better combination than the rabbit and the carrot? The rum is the Martinique touch. I put this recipe together after a trip to Martinique, and I guess I had rum on my mind.

   The beach plum sauce is very good with the pâté. I am very fortunate that the house here on Nantucket is surrounded with beach plum bushes. They are wonderful with any game dish.

Wine notes
Try a Zinfandel served on the cool side and see what you think.

Fish and Shellfish

Poisson Grillé aux Herbes

Grilled Fish with Herbs and a Tomato-Orange Fondue

Serves 2

1 whole two-pound fish (such as scup, bass, snapper, or a fresh water fish)
4 tablespoons olive oil
1 lemon
1 orange
6 sprigs parsley
1 branch thyme
1 bay leaf
1 branch rosemary
1 branch lavender
1 clove garlic, crushed

Fondue de tomates
2 large tomatoes
2 shallots, finely chopped
1 teaspoon olive oil
4 ounces unsalted butter
½ teaspoon chopped tarragon
½ teaspoon chopped parsley
3 anchovy filets, finely chopped

1. Make a marinade with the olive oil, the juice of half a lemon, the juice of half an orange, the parsley, thyme, bay leaf, rosemary, lavender, and garlic.
2. Scale the fish. Cut a small incision in the belly and remove the entrails. Remove the gills and cut off the fins and the tail. Wash and dry the fish. Salt and pepper. Put the fish in the marinade for 10 minutes, tossing it often.
3. Take the fish out of the marinade. Stuff the fish with the marinated herbs.
4. Cook the fish on the grill or barbecue – 8 minutes on each side should be sufficient.
5. Place the cooked fish on a plate. Garnish with assorted grilled peppers (see page 182). Serve with a fondue de tomates on the side (see below.)

Fondue de tomates

1. Blanch tomatoes for a few seconds in boiling water. Peel the tomatoes and cut them in half. Squeeze out the seeds. Cut the tomatoes into small dices.
2. Sauté the shallots in olive oil. Add the diced tomato, the juice of half a lemon, and the juice of half an orange. Cook for 5 minutes, then remove from heat. Whip in the butter. Add the tarragon, parsley, and anchovies. Taste for salt and pepper.

Grilled fish is always a popular dish anywhere. It is probably the oldest way of cooking, and it is still in vogue today. One of my favorite fish for grilling is sea bass or black bass – very tasty fish. I also like scup, or porgy. In France it is called *dorade,* a very popular fish. Make sure you remove all the scales, or they will burn and taste bitter. I also use fresh-water fish like white perch, also very tasty. Here we catch them in brackish water.

Wine notes
A nice crisp Chardonnay will do very well with the grilled fish. Keep the wine simple and on the young side.

Truite Farcie au Champagne

Stuffed Rainbow Trout with a Champagne Sauce

Serves 4

4 twelve-ounce trout
8 crayfish (or small shrimps)
9 ounces codfish
5 ounces of milk
3½ tablespoons unsalted butter
2¼ ounces flour
3 egg yolks
1 pinch nutmeg
3 egg whites
¼ cup chopped herbs (see below, step 3)
2 shallots, chopped
½ cup Champagne
½ cup heavy cream
2 tablespoons hollandaise (see page 89)
juice of ½ a lemon
1 tomato, peeled, seeded, and finely chopped

Panade
1. Put the milk and the butter in a small pot and bring to a boil. When the butter has melted, pull the pot away from the heat. Stir in the flour with a wooden spoon. When the flour is thoroughly mixed in, add the yolks, the nutmeg, and a pinch of salt. Place in refrigerator until cold.
2. Put the codfish in a food processor and run until smooth. Add egg whites, and salt and pepper to taste. Refrigerate.
3. The herb mixture should consist of 1 teaspoon of each of the following: chopped parsley, tarragon, mint, basil, chives, sorrel, chervil, and a sprig of thyme.
4. Take the cold panade and mix in the chopped herbs and the codfish purée, making sure that every ingredient is well blended in. Fill up a pastry bag with this forcemeat. Set aside.

Trout

1. Using a small knife and scissors, remove the backbone from the trout. Salt and pepper the trout. Fill it up with forcemeat. Reshape the fish and roll it in flour.

2. Place the trout in a sauté pan with a little butter. Cook it slowly for 5 minutes on each side, then bake it for 10 minutes at 350 degrees.

3. Remove the fish from the pan and discard the fat. Add chopped shallots and sauté for a minute. Add the Champagne, bring to a boil, and quickly reduce by half. Add the cream and boil until it starts to get thick. Take away from the heat and whip in the hollandaise. Add lemon juice, chopped tomato, salt and pepper to taste.

4. Place the trout on a warm plate. Remove the skin, pour the sauce around, and garnish with boiled crayfish.

A very elaborate and time-consuming recipe. It will tie you down in your kitchen for hours, but I could think of a lot worse places to be. The dish has a great combination of flavors and is also very attractive. If available, use fresh trout. Make sure you remove as many bones as possible.

Wine notes

I guess you could drink Champagne with this dish, but if you are like me, you like to drink your Champagne before or after dinner. It's always good anytime, but with food I prefer still wine. I would serve a Chardonnay on the mature side, four to five years old. I once had a 15-year-old Meursault-Genevrières with this trout. It was the right chemistry for me. The wine had a hint of maderisation. It was very smooth.

Beignets de Bluefish Timgad

Bluefish with a North African Flavor

Serves 4

2 pounds fileted bluefish
4 tablespoons olive oil
4 cloves garlic, crushed
2 hot peppers, cut up
peel of 1 whole lemon
1 tablespoon coriander seed
1 tablespoon cumin
1 pinch saffron
2 tablespoons grated ginger
6 mint leaves
1 pound tomatoes, peeled, seeded, and chopped
1 cup fish stock (see page 85)
¼ cup flour
2 eggs, beaten

1. In the blender, make a marinade with 1 cup of water, 3 tablespoons olive oil, the garlic, hot peppers, lemon peel, coriander seed, cumin, saffron, ginger, and mint leaves.
2. Cut the bluefish filets into scaloppini ¼ inch thick. Place the slices in the marinade for a few hours.
3. Sauté the chopped tomato in the remaining olive oil until cooked. Add the fish stock and 1 cup of the marinade. Taste for salt. Cook the sauce for 15 minutes. Put it in the blender and run until smooth. Set aside and keep warm.
4. Take the fish out of the marinade. Salt and pepper it. Dredge the scaloppini in flour and then dip them in beaten egg.
5. Sauté the scaloppini in olive oil for 2 minutes on each side. Serve with the tomato sauce.
6. Garnish with fried green pepper rings. (Cut a green pepper into slices. Dip each ring first in flour, then in the left-over beaten egg. Sauté in olive oil for approximately two minutes on each side. Drain on a towel.)

Here on Nantucket people get tired of bluefish. The fish are so abundant that you don't know what to do with them. I put this recipe together for people who don't even want to hear the word bluefish mentioned. This recipe has a North African influence, as I spent a couple of years in Algeria and got to taste a lot of their food – great couscous. I really like this dish, and I believe that I have converted even the most adamant non-lover of bluefish.

Wine notes
A Sauvignon Blanc from California or a Loire Valley wine would be my choice.

Quenelles de Bluefish au Tomates

Bluefish Quenelles with Tomato and Herb Sauce

Serves 6

2 pounds bluefish, fileted
2 cups milk
6 ounces unsalted butter
10 ounces flour
8 egg yolks
pinch of nutmeg
1 cup heavy cream
8 egg whites
2 quarts fish stock or water
2 cups tomato and herb sauce (see page 96: omit the orange peel)

Panade

1. Put milk and butter in a saucepan. Bring to a boil. Add salt, pepper, and nutmeg to taste. Thoroughly stir in the flour. Cook for a minute or two, then remove from heat.
2. Add the yolks one at a time. Refrigerate.

Bluefish

1. Grind up the bluefish very finely in the food processor. Put through a sieve if necessary.
2. Weigh the bluefish and return it to the food processor. Add the panade in the ratio of 9 ounces of panade to every 16 ounces of bluefish. Add heavy cream and 8 egg whites. Taste for seasoning.
3. Using 2 large spoons dipped in hot water, form scoops of the fish mixture into quenelles the shape and size of an egg.
4. Place the quenelles in a very wide roasting pan at least 3 inches deep. Pour boiling fish stock or boiling, salted water over the quenelles. Place the pan on medium heat. From this point on, the stock should not boil. Poach for 10 minutes.
5. When cooked, remove the quenelles with a slotted spoon and place them in a baking dish. Cover with tomato and herb sauce (see page 96). Bake for 8 to 10 minutes at 350 degrees.

This is a variation of the classical *quenelles de brochet* (pike quenelles). The bluefish quenelles are just as good, maybe even better.

Wine notes

Any of the white Côtes du Rhône, like Hermitage or Condrieu, will complement this dish.

Miroton de Cabillaud

Britanny Style Codfish Stew

Serves 4

4 pounds codfish
1 tablespoon olive oil
3 ounces unsalted butter
2 large onions, sliced thin
1 cup dry white wine
¾ cup chicken stock (see page 82)
3 ounces gherkins, cut into julienne (Make sure you use the sour kind.)
1 tablespoon capers
1 tablespoon chopped parsley

1. Clean and scale the fish. Cut into steaks 1½ inches thick. Pat dry on a paper towel.
2. In a skillet put the oil and one ounce of the butter. When hot, sauté the fish for 4 minutes on each side. Remove the fish and keep it warm. Add the thinly sliced onions. Keep stirring until brown. Add the wine, the stock, and salt and pepper to taste. Bring to a boil and reduce by half. Put the fish back in and cook slowly for 2 minutes. Remove the fish and put it on a platter.
3. Whisk in the remaining butter. Add the julienne gherkins, capers, chopped parsley. Spoon sauce over the fish.
4. I garnish this dish with ravioli stuffed with tomatoes and basil purée (see page 192).

I love codfish a lot. It's such an underrated and also a very versatile fish. I love the flaky white meat. I can't wait for April to go to Great Round Shoal and to catch a mess of them.

Wine notes
Serve a simple wine with this simple dish – a fruity Sauvignon Blanc or any of the Loire valley wines, like a nice Sancerre.

Beignets de Morue

Salt Cod Fritters

Serves 4

3½ ounces salt cod
6½ ounces flour
1 onion, finely chopped
1 clove garlic, finely chopped
5 whole scallions, finely chopped
1 sprig thyme, finely chopped
1 tablespoon finely chopped parsley
1 jalapeno or other hot pepper, finely chopped
2 eggs, separated
1 teaspoon red wine vinegar
1 teaspoon baking soda

1. Soak the salt cod in cold water for 3 to 4 hours. Rinse out the cod, cover it with water in a pot, and bring to a boil. Simmer for 20 minutes. Remove fish from water and set it aside to cool.
2. Put the flour in a bowl and, using a wire whip, slowly incorporate ½ cup water. Mix well.
3. Pick the salt cod to make sure there are no remaining bones and break it up into small pieces. Add the fish pieces and all the chopped ingredients to the flour and water mixture. Mix well. Add the egg yolks, vinegar, and baking soda; mix well again.
4. Beat the egg whites until they are firm and fold them into the mixture.
5. To deep fry the beignets, drop tablespoonfuls of the mixture into hot oil at about 350 degrees. (Use a skillet with about three inches of oil.) Only cook a few beignets at one time. Fry for about 5 minutes, until golden brown. Drain on paper towels. Serve with a sauce digoinaise (see page 90).

These beignets make a great lunch. I serve them with a salad of lamb's lettuce (mâche), endives, and cooked beets tossed in an oil, vinegar, and shallot dressing.

Wine notes
What better than a bottle of cool, crisp Muscadet or Gros Plant (seldom exported). They are the best white wines from Brittany.

Escalope de Flétan à l'Oseille

Scaloppini of Halibut in Sorrel Sauce

Serves 4

2½ pounds boneless halibut
8 leaves of spinach
8 oysters
1 cup fish stock (see page 85, or use clam juice)
1 tablespoon unsalted butter
2 shallots, finely chopped
3 ounces dry vermouth
½ cup heavy cream
16 leaves sorrel, shredded
2 tablespoons hollandaise (see page 89)

1. Wash the spinach leaves and blanch them for 2 minutes in boiling water. Drain and run under cold water to preserve the colour.
2. Open the oysters and put the juice in a small pan. Add the fish stock to the juice and bring to a boil. Drop the oysters in for a minute, and then take them out and wrap each one in a spinach leaf. Set aside.
3. Slice the halibut into thin slices ¼ inch thick. Lay the scaloppini on the table and salt and pepper them. Sauté them quickly in butter (2 minutes each side) and remove from pan. Discard the fat. Add the chopped shallots; sweat for a minute. Add the vermouth and bring to a boil. Pour in the cream and reduce by half. Add shredded sorrel, reserving some for garnish. Bring to a boil. Season to taste. Remove from heat and whip in the hollandaise.
4. Reheat the wrapped oysters in the hot fish stock for one minute. Drain on a towel.
5. Spread the sauce on the bottom of each plate and lay the scaloppini on top of it. Garnish with the oysters. Sprinkle a few shreds of sorrel on top.

This dish can also be done with other types of fish. I used to do it with striped bass, but when my favorite fish started to get into trouble, I never bought another striped bass again. You can use salmon, scup, or black bass.

Wine notes
I have tried many different wines with this dish and have experimented a lot. In any case, it has to be a full-bodied wine, not too high in acidity to compensate for the high acidity of the sorrel. I prefer a Chardonnay, maybe from Sonoma and at least four years old. I also like a Condrieu or a big white Graves, one of the better châteaux with a few years behind it.

Filets de Sole au Caviar

Filets of Sole with Caviar and Cucumber

Serves 4

8 filets of sole (I prefer grey sole)
1 small seedless European cucumber, peeled
2 cups fish stock (see page 85)
2 egg yolks
¼ cup heavy cream
1 teaspoon lemon juice
1 ounce unsalted butter
1 ounce caviar (Palaid sturgeon caviar, if available)

1. Cut the cucumber into very thin slices. Blanch in boiling water and keep crisp. Drain on a towel and set aside.
2. Butter the bottom of a shallow pan, lay in the filet of sole, cover with the fish stock (already hot), and cook slowly for 6 to 8 minutes. Remove from the pan and keep warm.
3. In a bowl mix together the egg yolks, the cream, the lemon juice, salt and freshly ground pepper. Whisk this mixture into the boiling poaching liquid. Remove at once from the heat. Whip in the butter and check the seasoning.
4. Cover the bottom of the platter with the sauce, arrange the filets of sole on top, cover the fish with the slices of cucumber, and sprinkle the caviar around the fish.

If possible, use grey sole. We get wonderful grey sole here; the flesh is very white and very firm. It reminds me of the sole we get in France. The flavor is also outstanding. It has to be, like all fish, very fresh. As I tell my apprentices in the kitchen, "If it smells fishy, throw it away." Fresh fish has no smell, just a sweet scent from the ocean.

Wine notes
Go wild. Treat yourself to a great Bâtard-Montrachet.

Sole au Pinot Noir

Filet of Sole Cooked in Red Wine

Serves 4

8 filets of sole (I prefer grey sole)
8 crayfish (or small shrimps)
2 cups red wine (use a Pinot Noir or a Côte du Rhône)
2 pounds fish bones (from a non-oily fish)
1 carrot, sliced
1 onion, sliced
1 stalk celery, sliced
1 bouquet garni
2 cloves garlic, crushed
3 shallots, chopped
1 tomato, chopped
1 clove
1 teaspoon glace de viande (see page 83)
juice of ½ lemon
1 teaspoon tomato paste
5 ounces unsalted butter
6 leaves shredded sorrel

1. Pour the wine into a saucepan (not aluminum). Bring it to a boil and flame it. Add one cup of water.
2. Wash the fish bones and chop them up.
3. Put a drop of olive oil in a sauteuse. Add the vegetables, the bouquet garni, the garlic, shallots, tomato, clove. Cook for a minute over high heat. Add the fish bones and the wine. Bring to a boil. Simmer for 30 minutes.
4. Strain the stock into another pot and reduce by one third. Add a teaspoon of glace de viande, a few drops of lemon juice, salt and freshly ground pepper to taste. Keep the sauce simmering slowly.
5. Salt and pepper the filets of sole. Sauté them quickly in butter for 3 minutes on each side. Take them out of the pan, put them on a plate, and keep warm.
6. Bring the sauce back to a boil and add tomato paste. Take it off the heat and whisk in the butter, a small amount at a time. Spoon the sauce over the sole filets. Garnish with the crayfish tails, previously sautéed in butter and taken out of their shells. Decorate with the shredded sorrel.
7. On the side of this sole, I serve ravioli stuffed with grapes, mushrooms, and spinach (see page 192).

Wine notes
A Pinot Noir, of course, young and served on the cool side. I might even go for a Beaujolais.

Lotte au Vinaigre de Miel

Monkfish Sautéed with Honey Vinegar

Serves 4

2½ pounds filet of monkfish
2 tablespoons unsalted butter
2 shallots, chopped
1 tablespoon red wine vinegar
1 teaspoon honey
4 tablespoons heavy cream
4 egg yolks

1. Cut the fish into slices ½ inch thick. Salt and pepper.
2. Put the butter in a sauté pan. When really hot, put in the slices of fish. Cook for 3 to 4 minutes on each side. Keep the fish warm between two plates.
3. Discard the leftover butter from the pan and put in the shallots and the vinegar. Bring to a boil and reduce until the vinegar has evaporated. Add the honey and cream. Mix with a wooden spoon, and let reduce for a minute. Keep warm.
4. Whip the yolks until they double their volume, and then incorporate the yolks into the sauce. Make sure the sauce is hot but do not let it boil. Taste for salt and pepper. Pour the sauce over the fish.
5. Garnish with cranberry and ginger crêpes the size of a half dollar. (See page 193 for basic recipe. Add 1 tablespoon fresh cranberries for every person and 1 teaspoon grated ginger for every 6 crêpes. Before adding the cranberries, cook them in the following manner: first boil one cup water with 2 tablespoons sugar for 5 minutes, then add the cranberries and cook for another 3 minutes.)

What a good fish. So versatile, it will pick up any of the flavors you cook with it.

Cooking with honey and vinegar is by no means a nouvelle cuisine method. It was used extensively in France during the Middle Ages. They used to distill honey and make a spirit called hydromel and a kind of vinegar called vergus. Both were used extensively.

Wine notes
Hermitage blanc would be my choice.

Homard et Lotte au Gingembre

Lobster and Monkfish in Ginger and Cream Sauce

Serves 4

1 two-pound lobster
1½ pounds monkfish
2 quarts court bouillon (see page 84)
2 cups heavy cream
1 ounce freshly grated ginger
1 tablespoon unsalted butter
1 egg
2 teaspoons olive oil
2 ounces marc de Bourgogne (see notes)
2 egg yolks

1. Boil the lobster in a court bouillon (see page 84) for 20 minutes. Remove from the pot and let cool. Remove the meat and save the shell and the head.
2. Pound the lobster head and shell with a rolling pin until mashed. Put in a saucepan with the cream, grated ginger, and salt and pepper to taste. Reduce slowly for 10 minutes. Strain, making sure to extract as much juice as possible by pressing hard on the shells. Keep warm.
3. Cut the monkfish into small, thin slices the size of a dollar piece. Salt and pepper. Dredge the pieces first in flour and then in the egg, previously beaten with one teaspoon olive oil. Sauté quickly in the remaining olive oil for two minutes on each side; keep warm.
4. Cut the lobster into thick scaloppini. Sauté briefly in butter and flame with the marc de Bourgogne.
5. Place the lobster in the center of a platter. Arrange the scaloppini of monkfish around it. Keep warm.
6. Finish the sauce by whipping the two egg yolks into it. Check seasoning.
7. Pour the sauce over the lobster. Glaze under the salamander or broiler for a second. Serve with wild rice risotto (see page 191).

An unusual combination, ginger and marc de Bourgogne. Marc is the distillation of wine residues (like stems, seeds, and skins) left after pressing. It's a very hearty brandy – a little rough, but a great flavor. In Italy it is called grappa. If you cannot find marc or grappa, I would substitute a brandy.

Wine notes
Serve a simple wine, not too complex. A white Châteauneuf-du-Pape seems appropriate. Because of the taste of ginger, I would probably have a Gewurztraminer or a Tokay d'Alsace.

Homard Rôti au Beurre de Champagne

Lobster Roasted Whole and Injected with Butter

Serves 4

4 one-and-a-quarter pound lobsters, live
4 ounces unsalted butter
4 shallots, chopped
2 cups Champagne
2 cups heavy cream
1 pinch saffron
2 tablespoons olive oil

1. In a heavy saucepan, put 1 tablespoon of butter and the shallots. Cook slowly until the shallots become translucent. Add the champagne and reduce by half. Add the cream, and salt and pepper to taste. Bring to a boil and reduce for about 5 minutes. Add the saffron. Whip in the butter. Strain the sauce through a fine strainer.
2. Fill up a large syringe (veterinarian type) with the sauce. Lay the lobsters on their backs and inject them first through the mandibles and then through the tail orifices with as much Champagne butter as possible.
3. Put the lobsters on a baking sheet. Paint them with olive oil. Bake at 400 degrees for 15 to 20 minutes.
4. Split lobsters in half. Serve remaining sauce on the side with wild rice risotto (see page 191).

I first learned to cook this dish at Charles Barrier's restaurant, where I was an apprentice in 1955. We used to get a small blue lobster from Brittany. (It's the same species as the Maine lobster.) I like this way of cooking lobster a lot, simply because no water or steam gets into the meat. The sweet flavor of the lobster meat is sealed in the shell with no dilution or loss of taste.

Wine notes
You need a great bottle of wine for this noble creature – a full-bodied, rich-flavored, buttery Chardonnay from California or a white Burgundy Grand Cru, a Puligny or a Chassagne.

Homard à la Crème au Gratin

Lobster Stewed in Cream and Herbs

Serves 4

2 three-pound lobsters
1 teaspoon olive oil
3 shallots, chopped
1 carrot, sliced
2 cloves garlic, chopped
3 ounces Cognac
1 cup dry white wine
1 large tomato, peeled, seeded, and chopped
1 teaspoon tomato puree
1 pinch cayenne pepper
½ teaspoon chopped tarragon
½ teaspoon chopped chives
1 tablespoon unsalted butter
9 ounces heavy cream
2 egg yolks

1. Put the olive oil in a heavy skillet. When warm, add the shallots, carrots, and garlic. Stir and cook at low heat for about 10 minutes.
2. Split the lobsters in half. Reserve the tomale in a little bowl. Discard the stomach.
3. Lay the lobsters, flesh side down, on top of the vegetables in the skillet. Cook for about 10 minutes at medium heat. Add the Cognac, white wine, tomatoes, tomato purée, cayenne, tarragon, chives, and 1 cup of cream. Cook for another 10 minutes, then remove the lobster and set it aside.
4. Take the lobster meat out of the shell and set aside. Take the lobster heads and crush them in a bowl. Add the crushed heads to the sauce. Cook for 5 minutes over low heat.
5. Strain the sauce into a saucepan. Bring to a boil and whip in the tomale. Remove from heat and whip in the butter. Beat the egg yolks with the remaining ounce of cream and add them to the sauce. Taste for salt and pepper.
6. Place the lobster meat (from tails and claws) in a skillet. Add a little butter and sauté quickly for 2 minutes.
7. Place the lobster on a heat-proof plate. Pour the sauce over the lobster. Glaze under the broiler until light brown.

Another aspect of lobster cookery. This dish is very festive – maybe serve it for a special dinner party. Take great care in removing the tomale from the lobster; the tomale is the ingredient that will give the sauce its velvety texture and reddish colour.

Wine notes
A great Chardonnay and a Corton-Charlemagne are the wines that come to mind with this elegant dish.

Homard Paillard

Sautéed Lobster in Port and Cognac Cream Sauce

Serves 2

1 wo-and-a-half pound lobster (can be boiled a day ahead)
2 tablespoons unsalted butter
2 ounces Cognac
6 ounces port
2 ounces whiskey
1 pinch cayenne pepper
12 ounces heavy cream
2 egg yolks
1 teaspoon lemon juice

1. Cook the lobster for 15 to 20 minutes in boiling, salted water. Let cool. Remove meat from tail and claws. Freeze head for lobster bisque.
2. Cut the lobster meat into medallions ¼ inch thick. In a heavy skillet, sauté in butter for about 2 minutes. Flame with the Cognac. Add the port and the whiskey. Season with salt and cayenne pepper. Cook slowly for 5 minutes.
3. Remove the lobster and reduce the cooking liquid by half.
4. Add the cream. Boil for a few minutes and then remove from heat.
5. Stirring constantly, add the egg yolks. Keep stirring and add the lemon juice and the remaining tablespoon of butter, a small amount at a time.
6. Spoon the sauce over the lobster and serve at once.

This preparation can also be done using a live lobster instead of boiled lobster meat. You would cut the carapace under the tail with scissors, remove the meat, and then cut the medallions. However, it's a lot more involved.

Wine notes
Serve a mature, full-bodied California Chardonnay or a Meursault Grand Cru.

Soufflé de Homard

Lobster Soufflé

Serves 4

1 three-pound lobster, live
1 carrot, diced
1 stalk celery, diced
2 shallots, chopped
1 teaspoon chopped chives
1 teaspoon chopped parsley
½ ounce truffle (if available)
2 ounces Cognac
½ cup dry white wine
1 cup heavy cream
4 ounces unsalted butter
¼ cup flour
1 cup milk
1 dash cayenne
4 egg yolks
5 egg whites

1. Remove the claws and the tail from the lobster. Do not separate the meat from the shell. Cut the tail into sections one inch thick. With a heavy knife smash the claws. (Leave the meat in the shell.) Save the head for making the sauce.

2. In a large saucepan make the following mirepoix (small diced vegetables). Melt a tablespoon of butter and add the carrot, celery, shallots, and chives. Cook over a very low heat until the vegetables are soft but not brown. Add parsley and truffles. Set aside.

3. In a sauté pan put a tablespoon of oil. When very hot, add the lobster pieces and let them get red all around (about 2 minutes on each side). Take the lobster out of the sauté pan and put the pieces on top of the mirepoix in the other pan. Flame with Cognac. Add white wine, cream, and salt and pepper to taste. Bring to a boil. Cook for 10 minutes over medium heat.

4. Remove the lobster pieces and carefully separate the meat from the shells. Cut the meat into slices ¼ inch thick.

5. Prepare the soufflé mixture as follows: Melt 3 tablespoons of butter in a saucepan. Add 3 tablespoons of flour and cook slowly until it starts to turn golden. Stir in 1 cup of boiling milk. Cook for about 5 minutes over low heat, stirring constantly. Add salt, pepper, and a dash of cayenne. Beat in 4 yolks. Bring to boiling point but do not boil.

6. Add the lobster meat and vegetable mixture to the soufflé base. Remove saucepan from heat. Fold in 5 egg whites, beaten stiff but not dry. Carefully pour into a buttered soufflé dish (1½ quart size). Cook at 375 degrees for 25 minutes.

7. Serve sauce chivry on the side (see page 93).

An involved recipe. A good holiday dish, soufflés are always a favorite with a lot of people because of the mystique associated with the dish. Soufflés are really not a complicated dish. Three key things to remember: 1. the consistency of the base should be on the thick side; 2. the egg whites should be whipped to perfection, stiff but not overwhipped (when they become grainy); 3. the oven temperature is crucial – not hot enough, the soufflé cooks but does not rise; too hot, the soufflé rises but does not cook inside.

Wine notes
Definitely a Chardonnay, as fat as they come.

Pithiviers de Homard, Sauce Cressonnette

Lobster and Vegetable Pie with a Watercress Sauce

Serves 4

one 2½ to 3 pound lobster (for 20 ounces of lobster meat)
8 ounces fresh spinach (about 3 tablespoons when cooked)
2 ounces unsalted butter
3 shallots, finely chopped
1 pinch nutmeg
6 medium mushrooms, chopped
½ teaspoon lemon juïce
1 small carrot, finely diced
1 stalk celery, finely diced
1 ounce Cognac
1 ounce port
1 ounce truffle juice (optional)
1 tablespoon heavy cream
1 pound puff pastry (frozen is fine)
1 egg, beaten for egg wash

1. Boil the lobster for about 15 to 20 minutes. Let it cool off. (The lobster may be cooked the day before.) Pick the meat and slice the large pieces into medallions about ¼ inch thick. Set aside.

2. Cook spinach in boiling water. When cooked, run under cold water. Drain and squeeze out the water.

3. Put a little butter in a small pan. Add ⅓ of the chopped shallots. Sauté for 2 minutes. Add the spinach, a pinch of nutmeg, and salt and pepper to taste. Slowly sauté the spinach for a minute or so. Set aside and keep warm.

4. Put a little butter in a small pan. Sauté the remaining chopped shallots. Add the chopped mushrooms, a few drops of lemon juice, and salt and pepper to taste. Bring to a fast boil and cook until the liquid has evaporated. Set aside.

5. Put a teaspoon of butter in a heavy skillet. Add the finely diced carrot and celery. Cook until tender. Lay the lobster slices on top of the vegetables. Flame with Cognac. Add port, truffle juice, and cream. Taste for salt and pepper. Bring to a boil. Remove the lobster meat and reduce by half.

6. Roll out the pastry ⅛ inch thick. Using a 9 inch plate, cut out a circle. Then, using a 10 inch plate, cut out another circle.

7. Lay the small circle on a sheet pan. Cover it to within 1 inch of the edge with the spinach, then the mushrooms, the carrots and celery, and finally the lobster. Put the 10 inch pastry cover on top. Seal the two covers together with egg wash. Pinch seam tightly.

8. Brush the top of the pithiviers with egg wash. Cut a small hole in the center so the steam can escape. Bake for 15 minutes at 375 degrees. Serve sauce cressonnette on the side (see page 94).

The pithiviers is usually a dessert, a wonderful cake of almonds, rum, and puff pastry. In this recipe I use the puff pastry and the shape of the cake, but the filling is a different story. Don't let the lobster overcook when you sauté it with the vegetables. Make it very quick.

Wine notes

A Chardonnay sounds good. Pick one rich enough to match this very flavorful dish. The watercress sauce can be tricky with a light white wine, but with California Chardonnays the way they are now, it should not be a problem.

Ecrevisses Grillées au Beurre Vert

Crayfish Grilled with Herb Butter

Serves 6

24 unshelled crayfish (or large shrimp)
3½ ounces unsalted butter
1 clove garlic, chopped
2 shallots, chopped
1 tablespoon chopped parsley
½ teaspoon chopped chives
½ teaspoon chopped tarragon
1 pinch cayenne pepper
2 ounces olive oil
1 ounce Calvados

1. Mix together the butter and the chopped herbs. Add the cayenne and set aside.
2. Using a small knife, split the crayfish as you would a lobster (belly up). Spread the crayfish open. Salt and pepper them.
3. Put the olive oil in a large iron sauté pan and set over high heat. When the oil is hot, put in the crayfish, flesh side down. Cook for 2 minutes, then flip over. Flame with Calvados.
4. Take the pan off the heat and spread the herb butter on top of each crayfish. Put the pan in the oven and cook for 4 minutes at 375 degrees.
5. Serve the crayfish immediately. Garnish with deep-fried parsley.

A fun appetizer or main course. Everyone will love it. Large shrimp can replace the crayfish.

Wine notes
Any kind of easy-drinking, unpretentious wine. Drink a fun wine, maybe a wine you have never tried before. There is always a bottle with which no one knows what to serve.

Coquilles St. Jacques Niçoise

Bay Scallops Sautéed with Tomatoes and Garlic

Serves 4

2 pounds bay scallops
3 medium, ripe tomatoes
3 tablespoons olive oil
8 mushroom caps, as white as possible
3 shallots, finely chopped
4 cloves garlic, finely chopped
2 ounces dry white wine
4 tablespoons flour (for dredging)
1 teaspoon chopped parsley
1 teaspoon chopped tarragon
1 teaspoon chopped basil
1 sprig thyme

1. Plunge the tomatoes into boiling water for a second. Remove the skin. Cut tomatoes in half and squeeze out the seeds. Cut the tomatoes into 1 inch cubes. Sauté them in a little olive oil for 3 to 4 minutes.
2. Cut the mushrooms into the same size cubes as the tomatoes. Sauté them with the chopped shallots and garlic in a little olive oil. Add the previously sautéed tomatoes and stew slowly for 2 minutes. Season with salt and pepper.
3. Pat the scallops dry with paper towels. Salt and pepper the scallops, then dredge them in flour.
4. Put the remaining olive oil (approximately 2 tablespoons) in a skillet. When hot, put the scallops in the pan and sauté quickly for 3 minutes; then add the tomatoes, mushrooms, white wine, and herbs. Stew for two minutes. Check for seasoning and serve right away.

A simple way to cook scallops. I had this recipe on the menu ten or twelve years ago, and to this day I have a customer who still asks for it. Keep the scallops undercooked.

Wine notes
A simple, unsophisticated wine for this dish. A Muscadet or a Chablis – steel dry.

Coquilles St. Jacques aux Légumes

Scallops Sautéed with Vegetables

Serves 4

24 ounces of scallops (bay scallops, if possible)
1 medium zucchini
2 tomatoes, peeled
2 tablespoons olive oil
6 medium mushrooms
1 tablespoon unsalted butter
2 shallots, chopped
1 clove garlic, chopped
2 artichoke bottoms, cooked and sliced (you can use canned bottoms)
1 teaspoon chopped parsley
¼ teaspoon chopped tarragon
¼ teaspoon chopped basil
½ teaspoon chopped chives

1. Cut the zucchini into bâtonnets (2 inches long by ½ inch wide). Blanch in boiling water until tender but still crisp. Set aside.
2. Cut the peeled tomatoes in half and squeeze out the seeds. Cut them into large dices and sauté in one teaspoon olive oil for 3 or 4 minutes. Set aside.
3. Cut the mushrooms the same size as the tomatoes. Sauté in butter and drain through a colander. Set aside.
4. Put the remaining olive oil in a large skillet. Let the oil get very hot. Add the scallops and sauté very fast for 2 minutes (until they start to get brown). Add the shallots and sauté for 1 more minute. Add tomatoes, mushrooms, zucchini, garlic, sliced artichoke bottoms, chopped herbs, salt and pepper to taste. Cook for 2 minutes.
5. Serve right away. Garnish with fresh pasta.

We are very privileged to live here on Nantucket, because when it comes to scallops, we have the best. They are so sweet, so pure and clean. Eat them raw, just plain with nothing on them; then you will know what I mean. You can use frozen ones – they freeze very well – but don't overcook scallops.

Wine notes
A fat, mellow Chardonnay will be very good.

Coquilles St. Jacques aux Poireaux

Stewed Scallops and Leeks

Serves 2

16 ounces scallops
1 large leek (white part only), cut into fine julienne
2 ounces unsalted butter
4 ounces mushrooms (use shiitake, if available), cut into julienne
2 shallots, chopped
2 ounces dry vermouth
3 ounces dry white wine
4 tablespoons heavy cream
1 teaspoon chopped chervil

1. Melt a little butter in a pan and add the leek julienne. Cook slowly for a few minutes.
2. Cook the mushrooms in the same way as the leeks.
3. Put a tablespoon butter in a large sauté pan. When melted and hot, add the scallops. Sauté at very high heat for 2 minutes.
4. Take the scallops out of the sauté pan and put them in a heavy-bottomed skillet. Add the chopped shallots, the vermouth, and the white wine. Bring to a boil and remove the scallops. Keep them warm.
5. Put the pan with the liquid back on the heat. Reduce by half. Add the cream and bring to a fast boil. Add the leeks and mushrooms. Let the sauce stand for a minute, then add salt and pepper to taste.
6. Pour the sauce over the scallops. Sprinkle with fresh, chopped chervil.

You could turn this into a kind of a stew by adding more cream and by not reducing it as much. Make sure you remove all of the green from the leeks because it becomes bitter when it cooks. A simple, fast, tasty dish – the kind I like.

Wine notes
A Fumé blanc from California or a Sancerre from the Loire region is a good match – maybe try one of each.

Pot-au-Feu de la Mer

Fish Stew with Vegetables

Serves 6

24 mussels
12 oysters
1 two-pound lobster
12 crayfish (or large shrimps)
1 pound scallops (preferably bay scallops)
1 pound fileted monkfish (or other firm fish)
1 small yellow turnip
½ gallon fish stock (see page 85)
3 carrots, peeled and cut into julienne
3 leeks (white part only), cut into julienne
3 stalks celery, cut into julienne
½ pound green beans
½ pound green peas
12 button mushrooms
½ bottle dry white wine
1 shallot, chopped
1 teaspoon chopped parsley
1 tablespoon beurre manié (softened butter and flour mixed in equal parts)
1 teaspoon lemon juice
½ cup heavy cream
1 teaspoon chopped basil

1. Using a tiny scoop, scoop out the turnip into little balls. Boil them in the fish stock until tender. When done, remove and set aside.
2. Blanch the carrot, leek, and celery julienne in the fish stock and set aside.
3. Boil the green beans and peas in fish stock for about 4 minutes. The beans and peas should still be crisp; be careful not to overcook. Remove and set aside.
4. Sauté the mushrooms in butter.
5. Steam the thoroughly scrubbed mussels in white wine with 1 chopped shallot and 1 teaspoon chopped parsley. Cook just until the mussels open. Remove from shell and set aside. Strain the mussel broth into the fish stock.
6. Open oysters and set aside. Save the oyster juice and strain it into the fish stock.
7. Boil lobster in salted water for 12 minutes. Remove lobster meat from shell and cut into slices ½ inch wide. Set aside. In the same water, boil the crayfish (or shrimp) for 3 minutes. Remove from shell and set aside.
8. Poach scallops in fish stock for 1 minute. Remove and set aside.
9. Poach oysters in fish stock for 1 minute. Remove and set aside.
10. Cut the monkfish into 1 inch squares. Poach in fish stock for 4 minutes. Remove and set aside.
11. Put 2 cups of the fish stock into a saucepan. Bring to a boil. Add 1 tablespoon beurre manié. Simmer for 5 minutes, stirring constantly with a wire whisk. Add the cream, salt, pepper, and 1 teaspoon lemon juice.

12. Combine all the vegetables into the sauce. Add the fish and shellfish. Bring to a quick boil. Sprinkle with chopped basil and serve immediately.

A nice fish combination. Keep the fish undercooked, as it will have to be reheated. You can also use salmon; it's very colourful.

Wine notes
Definitely a Chardonnay – rich, fruity, on the fat side, but not too oaky.

Moules Marinières

Mussels Steamed in Wine and Herbs

Serves 4

4 pounds mussels
5 ounces unsalted butter
6 shallots, chopped
1 cup dry white wine
1 bouquet garni
1 tablespoon chopped parsley

1. Put 3 tablespoons of the butter and the chopped shallots into a deep kettle. Sauté for a minute, then add the white wine and the bouquet garni. Simmer for 10 minutes.
2. Thoroughly scrub and wash the mussels. Put them in the kettle and cover. Bring to a boil, stirring occasionally until the mussels open.
3. Put the mussels in a dish. Sprinkle with chopped parsley and keep warm.
4. Strain the broth through a fine sieve. Return the broth to the heat and bring to a fast boil. Remove from heat and quickly whip in the remaining butter. Taste for salt and pepper. Pour the broth over the mussels. Garnish with garlic croutons (slices of French bread toasted and rubbed with garlic).

Where did moules marinières start? Either Brittany or Normandy, but who cares. It's such a perfect way to have mussels.

Wine notes
Simple wines – Muscadet, Fumé Blanc, maybe even a dry Riesling.

Oeufs de Caille et Huîtres en Meurette

Quail Eggs and Oysters Poached in Red Wine

Serves 4

12 quail eggs
24 oysters
½ bottle red wine
1 bouquet garni
1 onion, sliced
1 carrot, sliced
1 stalk celery, sliced
1 teaspoon tomato purée
1 clove garlic, crushed
1 tablespoon sugar
6 peppercorns
4 slices bacon, diced
3 mushrooms, diced
2 tablespoons unsalted butter
1 tablespoon flour
1 teaspoon chopped chervil (if unavailable, use chives)

1. Open the oysters and save the juices. Set aside.
2. Pour the wine into a saucepan. Add the bouquet garni, onion, carrot, celery, garlic, tomato purée, sugar, and peppercorns. Simmer for 30 minutes, then strain and return liquid to the pan.
3. Sauté the bacon and mushrooms. Strain to get rid of the extra fat. Set aside.
4. Bring the wine back to a gentle boil. Break the quail eggs one by one into a small bowl. Slip the eggs into the simmering wine. Cook for 2 minutes, then carefully remove the eggs with a skimmer. Set aside eggs and keep them warm.
5. Add the oysters and their juice to the red wine reduction. Cook just until the oysters start to curl. Remove the oysters from the sauce and drain them on a towel.
6. Make a beurre manié by working the soft butter and flour together into a paste. Skim the wine reduction to remove any pieces of egg white. Return the wine to the heat and bring to a boil. Add the beurre manié, stirring with a whisk until the sauce thickens. Add bacon and mushrooms. Taste for salt and pepper.
7. Arrange the quail eggs and oysters on 4 separate plates (one egg, two oysters, etc.) Pour the sauce over the oysters but not over the eggs. Sprinkle with chopped chervil. You can also garnish the center of each plate with a few leaves of spinach quickly sautéed in butter.

Wine notes
A Nantucket version of an old Burgundian dish. It makes me feel like a long, wintery Sunday lunch with good friends and a few bottles of wine – maybe a Beaujolais Nouveau, – when it first arrives here in late November.

Crevettes et Moules au Curry

Light Curry of Shrimp and Mussels

Serves 4

2 pounds mussels, scrubbed and washed
16 large shrimps, peeled and deveined
2 tablespoons olive oil
1 medium onion, chopped
1 stalk celery, diced
1 apple, peeled, cored, and diced
curry powder to taste (I use about 1 teaspoon per person)
1 large tomato, peeled, seeded, and diced
1 clove garlic, chopped
2 tablespoons heavy cream
1 tablespoon raisins
grated ginger
2 green onions, thinly sliced

1. Cook the mussels like you would for moules marinières (see steps 1 and 2 of recipe on page 147). Save the broth. Take the mussels out of the shell and set aside.
2. Put a teaspoon of olive oil in a skillet. Add the onions, celery, and apple. Sauté quickly for 2 or 3 minutes. Add the curry powder to taste. Add the diced tomatoes, the garlic, and the mussel broth. Bring to a boil and simmer for 5 minutes.
3. Sauté the shrimps in a little olive oil until they get brown. Add the shrimps to the curry sauce. Add the cream and the raisins. Bring to a boil and add the mussels.
4. Serve as soon as the mussels are hot. Sprinkle grated ginger and sliced green onion on top. Garnish with fresh pasta.

This preparation was very well received when I put it on the luncheon menu last year. It's a very mild curry. (I am not fond of very hot food; I like to taste what I eat.) If you like your food hotter, by all means increase the amount of curry powder.

Wine notes
With curry I like the spiciness of a Gewurztraminer, but any simple white wine will go well.

Bourguignon de Grenouilles et Crevettes

Frog Legs and Shrimp Stewed in Red Wine

Serves 4

2 pounds frog legs
1 pound large shrimps, peeled and deveined
8 button mushrooms
8 pearl onions
4 ounces thick bacon
1 carrot, peeled
1 leek (white part only)
1 tablespoon olive oil
2 tablespoons flour (for dredging)
2 ounces Cognac
2 cups red wine
1 clove garlic, crushed
1 bouquet garni
1 tomato, peeled, seeded, and diced
1 tablespoon glace de viande (see page 83)
1 pinch sugar
1 teaspoon chopped tarragon

1. Wash mushrooms and sauté them quickly in butter. Set aside. Repeat the same process with the pearl onions.
2. Cut the bacon into lardons ½ inch square. Blanch in boiling water for 2 minutes. Drain. Lightly sauté the lardons until brown. Drain fat and set lardons aside.
3. Using a tiny scoop, make little balls out of the carrot. Blanch the carrot balls for a few minutes. Drain and set aside.
4. Thoroughly wash and rinse the leek. Slice thinly and set aside.
5. Lay frog legs and shrimp on a table. Salt and pepper them, then dredge them in flour. In a skillet, quickly sauté the frog legs and shrimp in olive oil until brown.
6. Remove frog legs and shrimp from skillet and place them in a non-corrosive pot. Flame with Cognac. Add red wine and bring to a boil. Add onions, carrot balls, crushed garlic, bouquet garni, and diced tomatoes. Cook slowly until frog legs are tender.
7. Remove frog legs and shrimp from pot and keep them warm between two plates. Add mushrooms, lardons, and leeks to the stew. Bring to a boil and simmer for 5 minutes. Add glace de viande and a pinch of sugar. Taste for seasoning.
8. When the sauce starts to thicken, put the frog legs and shrimp back in the pot. Stew for 5 minutes. Serve with fresh pasta sprinkled with chopped tarragon.

I think this is one of my biggest dishes. By that I mean one with the most intense flavors and concentration of flavors. I like to use small frog legs from Louisiana and large Gulf shrimps.

Wine notes
Time for a big red wine. A Côte-Rôtie from the Rhône region or an Hermitage, also from that region. A Zinfandel will also stand up very well.

Game Birds
and
Poultry

Canard Rôti au Châteauneuf-du-Pape

Roast Duck with a Red Wine Sauce

Serves 2

1 three-pound duck, as lean as possible
6 juniper berries
4 sprigs thyme
2 tablespoons cooking oil
1 small onion, sliced
1 clove garlic, crushed
½ bottle red wine (Chateauneuf-du-Pape preferred)
2 shallots, chopped
2 ounces Cognac
1 teaspoon tomato paste
1 duck liver, finely chopped
2 tablespoons unsalted butter

1. Cut the neck and wings off the duck. Set aside.
2. Salt and pepper the duck inside and out. Stuff the bird with the juniper berries and the thyme. Rub the duck with a little oil.
3. Chop up the neck and wings and place the pieces in a roasting pan. Add onion and garlic. Place the duck on top of the chopped pieces. Roast for 10 minutes at 425 degrees and then for 25 minutes at 350 degrees. Remove the duck from the pan and set aside.
4. Add the red wine to the pan. Place the pan on the heat and let simmer at low heat.
5. Cut the legs off the duck and cook them under the broiler for 10 minutes or until crisp on both sides. Remove the breasts from the duck and keep them warm.
6. Chop up the duck carcass and reserve the pieces. In a deep pan or large skillet, put the remaining oil. When hot, add the shallots and the chopped-up duck bones. Sauté for a minute or two. Add the Cognac, the tomato paste, and the previously cooked red wine stock. Boil for 5 minutes, then strain. Return the strained sauce to the heat and add the finely chopped liver. Bring to a boil, and then strain again. Whip in the butter. Season with salt and pepper.
7. Slice the duck breasts and arrange the slices on a plate with the broiled legs. Pour the sauce around the duck.

When slicing the breast, cut it on an angle and make the slices ¼ inch thick. If you have an open grill (barbecue type), the legs will taste even better. Let the legs cook all the way, till crisp and almost dry. The pink, tender breasts and brown, crisp legs make a nice contrast.

Wine notes
Châteauneuf-du-Pape, an older one, would be my choice. Otherwise, I would say a Cabernet.

Pot-au-Feu de Canard, Sauce Moutarde

Salt-Cured Duck Boiled with Vegetables
and Served with a Mustard Sauce

Serves 4

2 four-pound ducks
1 pound rock salt
3 large carrots
4 stalks celery
1 medium onion
1 bouquet garni
2 cloves
6 peppercorns
2 cloves garlic
1 small yellow turnip
1 medium zucchini
1 medium cucumber
2 leeks (white part only)
3 ounces flour
2 tablespoons Dijon mustard
1 teaspoon dry mustard
½ teaspoon horseradish

1. Cut the wings off the duck and set aside. Remove first the breasts and then the legs from the carcasses. Lay breasts and legs in a pan. Cover with rock salt and marinate in the refrigerator for 24 hours.
2. Using the duck carcasses, make a stock. Put the carcasses in a large pot. Cover with water and bring to a boil. Skim the top. Add one sliced carrot, one sliced celery stalk, one sliced onion, a bouquet garni, 2 cloves, a few peppercorns, and 2 cloves of garlic. Cook slowly for 3 hours. (The marinade and the stock should be prepared a day ahead.)
3. Strain the stock through a china cap and return it to the pot. Keep stock warm.
4. Cut all the remaining vegetables, except for the leeks, into bâtonnets 2 inches long by ½ inch wide. Trim the root ends and the green tops off the leeks. Leave the leeks whole. (Rinse them thoroughly.)
5. Thoroughly rinse the duck breasts and legs under cold water. Put the legs and all the vegetables in the stock. Bring to a boil. Cook for 20 minutes, then add the breasts. Cook for an additional 10 to 15 minutes. Remove the duck pieces and the vegetables from the stock pot and keep them warm in another pan with a little of the stock.
6. Remove the fat floating on top of the stock and put 3 tablespoons of the fat into a small sauce pan. Add the flour and cook for a few minutes. Add two cups of the duck stock and let it reduce until it reaches the consistency of heavy cream. Whip in both mustards and the horseradish. Check for salt and pepper.
7. Serve on individual plates. Put the sauce on the bottom, then the breast and the leg. Arrange the vegetables around the duck.

Another great fall or winter favorite. I truly love this dish, and so do many of my friends. The pot-au-feu will make you feel warm on the coldest day. Plan on half a duck per person. Make sure to rinse the duck very thoroughly after marinating, or it will be too salty. The dry mustard in the sauce adds an extra bite.

Wine notes
A nice bottle of Pomerol is a great companion to this duck. A Cabernet Sauvignon or a Merlot will also be terrific.

Magret de Canard Grillé au Genièvre, Sauce Cumberland

Grilled Duck Breast with Juniper Berries and a Currant Sauce

Serves 4

4 boned duck breasts, skin left on
12 juniper berries
2 tablespoons olive oil
½ cup red wine
1 teaspoon honey
1 shallot, chopped
1 bouquet garni
1 clove garlic, chopped
Cumberland sauce (see page 91)

1. Toast the juniper berries in the oven at 400 degrees for 2 minutes. Crush them up and sprinkle over the duck breasts. Place the breasts in a non-corrosive dish, and salt and pepper them. Add olive oil, red wine, honey, the chopped shallot, the bouquet garni, and the chopped garlic. Marinate in the refrigerator for 24 hours.
2. Remove the magrets from the marinade. Dry them on a paper towel. Cook on a hot grill, skin side down first, for 5 minutes on each side. Do not overcook. The magret should be quite pink inside.
3. Remove the whole skin from the magret and crisp it up on the grill. Slice the magret into thin slices and arrange the slices on a plate.
4. Garnish with the crisped magret skin and corn custard (see page 185). Serve with a Cumberland sauce (see page 91).

Duck is probably my favorite game bird. I like everything about ducks: hunting them, cooking them, eating them, collecting antique duck decoys, and carving decorative decoys. I use Muscovy ducks raised here on Nantucket for all of my duck recipes. They have large breasts and are very tasty. You can use any kind of duck – just keep them rare.

Wine notes
A red Burgundy is a must. I would have a Côte de Beaune – an old-style Beaune, thick and sturdy. Maybe a Corton, maybe even a '69 or '72. Heaven!

Magret à l'Aigre Doux

Sautéed Duck Breast with a Vinegar and Honey Sauce

Serves 4

4 duck breasts (magrets), boned and skinned
2 cups red wine
1 tablespoon chopped parsley
1 tablespoon olive oil
½ teaspoon coriander seed
1 tablespoon chopped shallots
2 ounces red wine vinegar
1 tablespoon honey
1 tablespoon heavy cream

1. Marinate the boneless magrets in red wine, parsley, olive oil, and coriander seeds for 24 hours in the refrigerator.
2. Remove the magrets from the marinade and dry them well with a paper towel. Salt and pepper them. Reserve the marinade.
3. In a sauté pan, melt some unsalted butter. Sauté the magrets for 4 to 5 minutes on each side. Keep the breasts rare. Set aside and keep warm.
4. Discard the fat from the pan and add a little butter. Add the shallots and cook for 2 minutes. Deglaze the pan with the vinegar. Add ¼ cup of the marinade. Reduce by one third. Add the honey and the heavy cream. Bring to a boil and check the seasoning.
5. Slice each magret into 6 slices. Pour some sauce onto each plate and place the magret slices on top of the sauce.

A magret with a different touch – sweet and sour – and with a sauce on the lighter side. A sautéed breast will have a different texture than a grilled one, and the flavors will not be as aggressive.

Wine notes
A Pinot Noir with good fruit and body will go well. A Cabernet Sauvignon will also do well, but choose one on the softer side, not too tannic but with lots of fruit.

Cuisses de Canard Farcies au Vin Rouge

Stuffed Duck Legs Stewed with Vegetables and Red Wine

Serves 6

6 duck legs
8 ounces boned pork (about 60% lean)
2 shallots, chopped
1 clove garlic, chopped
1 bay leaf, chopped
1 pinch thyme
2 eggs
2 tablespoons Armagnac
2 carrots, diced
1 leek (white part only), sliced
1 medium red onion, chopped
2 ounces Madeira
1½ cups red wine
¼ cup raisins
¾ cup demi-glace (see page 83)
1 teaspoon green peppercorns (optional)

1. Using a sharp boning knife, cut the bone out of each duck leg. Do not puncture the skin; just pull it gently away from the meat. Save the skins. Use the bones for stock.
2. Grind up the duck meat and the pork. Add shallots, garlic, bay leaf, thyme, eggs, Armagnac, salt and pepper to taste. The mixture should be coarse but even.
3. Stuff the skins and shape them like duck legs. Tie them with pieces of string if necessary.
4. Over medium heat, sauté the legs in a skillet with a touch of butter. When brown on all sides, remove the legs. Add carrot, leek, and onion. Sauté for 5 minutes at medium heat, stirring constantly.
5. Put the duck legs on top of the vegetables. Flame with the Madeira. Add the red wine and the raisins. Bring to a boil. Cover the pan and put it in the oven. Cook for 30 minutes at 375 degrees.
6. Remove the duck legs from the pan and keep them warm. Add demi-glace to the pan and bring to a boil. Taste for salt and pepper. You can also add a teaspoon of green peppercorns. Reduce the sauce by one third.
7. Slice the duck legs crosswise in ½ inch thick slices. Arrange them on individual plates and spoon the sauce over the top. Serve fresh pasta on the side.

Enormous flavor in this preparation. This is a fine way to accommodate duck legs if you have some spare ones in your freezer and you don't want to make confit. If you use very large duck legs, you may have to cook them for more than 30 minutes.

Use a decent bottle of wine for cooking. Remember, the quality of the wine you use for a sauce will reflect in the end product.

Wine notes
Châteauneuf-du-Pape comes to mind with this sturdy dish.

Confit de Canard

Preserved Duck

Serves 4

8 duck legs
5 cups rendered duck fat or rendered chicken fat (your butcher can easily order it for you.
  Goose fat is also very good for confit.)
rock salt (1 tablespoon per pound of duck)
2 shallots, chopped
2 tablespoons chopped parsley
2 teaspoons crushed peppercorns
1 bay leaf, chopped
1 sprig thyme
2 cloves garlic, chopped
4 cloves garlic, crushed
2 cloves

1. Trim the fat from the duck legs. Weigh the legs and place them in a stainless steel bowl. Add 1 tablespoon rock salt per pound of duck. Add the shallots, parsley, peppercorns, bay leaf, thyme, and 2 cloves of chopped garlic. Toss all the ingredients for a minute or two. Cover the bowl with plastic wrap and refrigerate for 24 hours.
2. Remove the duck legs from the marinade. Rinse them thoroughly under cold water. Dry the legs in a paper towel.
3. Place the rendered duck fat in a large heavy pan. Put on the heat and bring the temperature of the fat up to 190 degrees Fahrenheit.
4. Lay the duck legs in the hot fat, making sure that they are completely covered. Bring the temperature of the fat back to 190 degrees. Add the cloves and the crushed garlic.
5. Place the pan with the fat and the legs in an oven preheated to 190 degrees. Cook until the meat pulls easily off the bone (about 2 hours). Make sure that the temperature remains at 190 degrees during the cooking process.

6. Remove the legs from the fat and place them in a bowl. Bring the fat to a boil. Skim off the top. Keep simmering for 5 minutes. Remove from heat and let cool for a while. Ladle the fat over the duck, making sure that duck is completely covered.

7. Refrigerate when cold. The confit will then keep for weeks.

8. When ready to serve, take the confit out of the refrigerator and let the fat soften up. Carefully pull the duck legs out of the fat. Grill the legs on a hot grill for 3 minutes on each side. They should be crisp and free of fat.

9. Serve with apple fritters (see page 188).

This method of preserving meat is one of the oldest preparations. It is used extensively in the Dordogne region, one of my favorite parts of France. Confit is time-consuming but worth every minute invested in its preparation. I like duck legs for confit; I reserve the breasts for grilled or sautéed magret. When you make confit, make a lot of it. If refrigerated, it will keep in the fat for a couple of months. A good garnish for confit is wild mushrooms sautéed with garlic, shallots, and parsley.

Wine notes

If you can, drink a red wine from the Southwest of France – fruity, uncomplicated, and young. Choose one high in alcohol like a Bergerac, which is made from the Malbec grape.

Cailles Grillées à la Confiture d'Airelles

Grilled Quail with a Cranberry and Red Wine Preserve

Serves 4

8 quails
2 cloves garlic, crushed
½ teaspoon herbes de Provence (available at gourmet shops)
½ cup olive oil
1 ounce unsalted butter
4 shallots, chopped
½ cup chicken stock (see page 82)
1 teaspoon Dijon mustard
1 teaspoon lemon juice
dash Worcestershire sauce

Compote d'airelles et d'oignons

8 ounces red onions, chopped
1 ounce sugar
4 tablespoons red wine
1 tablespoon red wine vinegar
4 ounces cranberries

1. Split the quails down the back and gently flatten each with the side of the cleaver.
2. In a bowl, mix the garlic, herbes de Provence, pinch of salt and pepper, and olive oil. Rub quails with marinade. Let them stand in the marinade for 2 hours, turning from time to time.
3. Put the quails, breast side down, on a hot grill for 3 minutes and keep basting them with the oil marinade. Turn over every two minutes, basting with oil until they are cooked (about 10 minutes altogether).
4. While the quails are cooking, prepare the following sauce. Put a little butter in a small sauce pan. Sauté the shallots for a minute or two, then add the chicken stock and the mustard. Reduce the sauce by one third. Add the lemon juice and a few drops of Worcestershire sauce.
5. Serve the quails on a hot platter with the sauce on the side. Garnish with compote d'airelles et d'oignons (see below).

Compote d'airelles et d'oignons

1. Melt a little butter in a pan with a very heavy bottom. Add the onions, sugar, and salt and pepper to taste. Cover and cook slowly for half an hour.
2. Add the red wine, the vinegar, and the cranberries. Cook for another 15 minutes. Serve warm.

An enormous dish by its flavor. Use bobwhite quails if you can get them; they are so tasty and so plump.

Wine notes
This is the perfect dish for Zinfandel, or any young Cabernet Sauvignon.

Faisan aux Endives

Pheasant Stewed with Endives

Serves 4

2 pheasants, cut in quarters
3 ounces Calvados
1 cup Sauternes
8 medium mushroom caps
1 cup heavy cream
½ lemon
3 medium endives, cut crosswise into 1 inch thick slices
8 morels (if unavailable, use shiitake mushrooms)
½ cup seedless white grapes (optional)

1. Salt and pepper the pheasant quarters. Sauté them in butter. When brown on all sides, remove pheasant pieces from pan and discard all the fat.
2. Return the pheasant to the pan and flame with the Calvados. Remove the breasts but leave the legs in the pan. Add the Sauternes, the mushroom caps, and the heavy cream. Bring to a boil. Add the lemon juice and the cut-up endives. Cook slowly.
3. When the endives feel soft, add the breasts and cook for about 10 minutes.
4. Remove all the pheasant pieces from the pan and add the morels. (You can also add ½ cup seedless white grapes.) Bring to a boil and season with salt and pepper.
5. Pour the sauce over the pheasant. Serve with wild rice.

I serve this dish to a lot of my friends when we have dinner at the house. We usually have six guests, so I save four birds from two days of hunting (two birds a day). I age them for four days because I don't want them to taste too strong. The wild pheasants that we get here taste so special to me. They eat a lot of berries – cranberries, blueberries, beach plums, even bayberries. That is why they taste so special. I also pick wild mushrooms (mostly bolets) on the moors while pheasant hunting, so I use them for this recipe. Everyone seems to love this stew; it's different. I also serve slices of apple sautéed in butter.

Wine notes
Since I use a lot of cream in this dish, I might go with a white wine – a rich, full-bodied white Graves from one of the better chateaux.

Faisan Farci aux Herbes

Pheasant Stuffed with Ricotta, Bacon, Mushrooms, and Herbs

Serves 4

four 14-ounce pheasants or cornish hens
2 ounces unsalted butter
½ pound bacon
juice of one lemon
4 tablespoons chopped parsely
1 tablespoon chopped chives
1 teaspoon chopped tarragon
½ pound mushrooms, quartered
4 shallots, chopped
½ pound ricotta
1 tablespoon red wine vinegar
½ cup chicken stock (see page 82)
3 tablespoons heavy cream
1 small tomato, peeled, seeded, and finely chopped
1 teaspoon chervil (if available)

1. In the food processor put together the butter, bacon, lemon juice, 1 tablespoon of water, and salt and pepper to taste. Run for a minute. Add the parsley, chives, tarragon, mushrooms, 3 of the shallots, and the ricotta. Run processor again until the mixture looks like a paste.
2. Take each bird and, starting from the neck side, very carefully lift the skin from the body with your fingers. Make sure you do not puncture the skin or remove it completely.
3. Take some stuffing and carefully push it in the space between the skin and the flesh. Pay special attention to the breast and the legs.
4. Put the birds in a roasting pan. Cook for 10 minutes in the oven at 400 degrees and then for 25 minutes at 350 degrees.
5. Take the birds out of the pan and discard any fat left in the pan. Add the last shallot and cook for one minute over medium heat. Deglaze the pan with vinegar and reduce. Add the chicken stock and the cream. Bring to a boil and let it cook for a minute or two. Add the finely chopped tomato. If available, add a teaspoon of chopped chervil.
6. Serve with corn and spinach crêpes (see page 193).

What an exciting preparation. A little time consuming, perhaps, but well worth it, and great for the holidays. The meat of the bird will be so moist! Be careful when you stuff the bird not to rip the skin. Take your time.

Wine notes
With game I like a red Burgundy. With this dish I would probably have a wine from the Côte de Nuits. If white were preferred, I would have a Condrieu.

Poulet Rôti Nantaise

Roast Chicken, Brittany Style

Serves 2

1 two-and-a-half pound chicken
½ bottle Muscadet
3 ounces Madeira
1 carrot, sliced
1 tablespoon unsalted butter
½ tablespoon flour
3 shallots, chopped
1 clove garlic, chopped

1. Prepare a marinade with the Muscadet, the Madeira, the sliced carrot, salt, and pepper. Place the chicken in the marinade. After two hours, remove the chicken. Drain and dry it. Strain the marinade and set aside.
2. Put the chicken in a heavy skillet. Brush it with oil and sprinkle a little salt and pepper over it. Roast the chicken at 375 degrees for 40 minutes.
3. Remove the chicken from the pan and cut it up into 4 pieces. Keep warm and set aside.
4. Add the butter to the pan. When melted, add the flour. Mix with a whip and cook for 2 minutes. Pour in the strained marinade. Keep stirring. Add the shallots and garlic. Cook slowly for 10 minutes.
5. Put the chicken back in the sauce. When warm, serve with potatoes roasted in bacon fat.

This brings back childhood memories. We used to have this chicken on Sundays. I think I remember the recipe pretty well, or close to it. My grandfather kept chickens in the garden, and we used to slaughter one every Saturday. They were huge chickens; maybe they were capons. You could feed six people from one chicken and also make a soup from the neck, feet, and wings.

Wine notes

I don't remember what the grown-ups drank then, but it must have been red. The treat for us kids was to have a drop of red wine in our water. Today, I would probably have a Grand Cru Beaujolais, maybe a Morgon or a Chiroubles.

Poulet au Vinaigre et Basilic

Roast Chicken with Vinegar and Basil Sauce

Serves 4

four 14 to 16 ounce poussins (baby chickens, or use Cornish hens)
7 ounces unsalted butter
4 bunces Armagnac
¼ cup vinegar (if possible, use balsamic vinegar)
4 ounces Prosciutto, diced
8 leaves tarragon
4 leaves basil
6 mushrooms, diced
½ cup demi-glace (see page 83)
1 teaspoon chopped parsley

1. Salt and pepper the cornish hens. Put a pat of butter on each. Place in a heavy sauteuse or a heavy cast-iron skillet. Roast in the oven at 400 degrees for 30 minutes, basting and turning often.
2. Sauté the mushrooms in a teaspoon of butter. Set aside.
3. Take the birds out of the pan. Discard the fat. Put the birds back in and flame with Armagnac. Add the vinegar. Add the prosciutto, tarragon, basil, and mushrooms.
4. Clarify and decant the remaining butter. Mix it with the demi-glace. Pour this mixture over the birds. Put them back in the oven for 5 minutes.
5. Split the birds in half and arrange them on a platter. Taste the sauce for salt and pepper. Pour sauce over the birds. Sprinkle with chopped parsley. Serve with potato and leek pancakes (see page 190).

The original recipe was for guinea hen, a very tasty bird. My friend Stephen Swift used to raise them for me on Nantucket. If you have a chance to find guinea hens, by all means use them instead of poussins or Cornish hens. Balsamic vinegar is very important in this preparation; the other vinegars are too sharp.

Wine notes
Cabernet Sauvignon, sturdy and young.

Poularde Pochée à l'Estragon

Chicken Poached in Tarragon Consommé

Serves 4

1 four-pound hen
2 bunches tarragon
3 quarts chicken stock (see page 82)
2 cucumbers
2½ cups heavy cream
2 egg yolks
1 teaspoon lemon juice

1. Pick out the leaves from ½ bunch of tarragon. Blanch them in boiling water for a second. Remove and put in iced water to cool, then set aside on a towel.
2. Put ½ bunch of tarragon inside the hen. Put the chicken stock into a large kettle and add the last bunch of tarragon to it. Bring stock to a boil.
3. Place the hen into the kettle and cover with a kitchen towel. Cook slowly for about one hour.
4. Peel and seed the cucumbers. Turn them into small pieces the size and shape of an olive. Blanch in boiling water and keep crisp.
5. Put the cream in a saucepan and bring it to a boil. Reduce by one third. Add the blanched tarragon leaves, remembering to save a few for decoration. Taste for salt and pepper. Keep warm.
6. Sauté the cucumber pieces in a little butter but do not brown.
7. In a bowl whip the two egg yolks with a tablespoon of warm chicken stock. When fluffy, whip in the reduced cream and the lemon juice, a small amount at a time. Check the seasoning. Return to heat and cook gently like an egg custard for 2 to 3 minutes.
8. Cut the hen into quarters and remove the skin. Place the pieces on a platter. Arrange the cucumbers around the chicken. Pour the sauce over the fowl and decorate with blanched tarragon leaves. Garnish with fresh pasta.

A nice way to prepare a chicken, this dish can be done ahead and reheated. The sauce has to be done à la minute. Dry tarragon can be substituted if fresh is not available, but it will not taste the same.

Wine notes
A Sauvignon Blanc or a white Graves will go very well with this dish.

Ailerons de Poulet au Meursault

Boned Chicken Wings Stewed in Wine with Cucumbers

Serves 4

40 chicken wings
2 medium cucumbers, peeled
2 ounces unsalted butter
4 ounces diced mushrooms
2 shallots, chopped
2 ounces dry vermouth
5 ounces dry white wine (if possible use Meursault)
¾ cup heavy cream
2 tomatoes, peeled, seeded, and diced
½ teaspoon chopped tarragon
1 teaspoon chopped chervil
1 teaspoon sugar

1. Cut the wings into their three sections. Only keep the central part for this recipe. Use the meatiest section and the tip section for making stock.
2. Blanch the wings in boiling water for 3 or 4 minutes. Remove from water and let cool.
3. Pull the two bones out of the wings.
4. Cut the cucumbers into pieces 1½ inches long. Split them in four and remove the seeds. Round off each piece so it looks like a large olive. Blanch the turned cucumber in boiling water for 3 minutes. Set aside.
5. In a heavy skillet, put one ounce of butter. When hot, add the boned chicken wings. Add salt and pepper to taste. Cook slowly, turning over once in a while, for about 10 minutes. Remove chicken from the pan and set aside.
6. Put diced mushrooms and shallots in the same pan used for the chicken. Sauté for 4 minutes. Add vermouth and white wine. (Use Meursault, if possible, and then serve the rest of the bottle with the dish.) Reduce liquid by half. Add the cream, the finely diced tomato, the tarragon, and the chervil. Bring to a boil and reduce for a minute. Add the chicken wings. Keep warm but do not boil.
7. Sauté the cucumbers in the remaining butter. Add the sugar. Roll the cucumber pieces in the pan so that they get brown all over.
8. Put the wings and sauce onto individual plates. Garnish with the cucumbers. Serve fresh pasta on the side.

The recipe sounds complicated, but really it's not. It is a little time-consuming, but I guarantee the result: the best chicken wings you ever had, and also an inexpensive dish.

Wine notes
A Meursault-Charmes would be heaven. You could even use the Meursault in the recipe, then finish the bottle with the dish.

Boudins Blancs de Dinde Grillés

Turkey Sausages, Grilled and Served with Apples

Serves 6

17 ounces turkey breast, trimmed
14 ounces unsalted fatback
3½ ounces chopped onion
1 teaspoon unsalted butter
1 sprig thyme
1 bay leaf
2 cups milk, boiled and cooled
1 tablespoon chopped truffle (if available)
1 pinch nutmeg
4 egg whites
sausage casing (ask your butcher for a piece of Italian sausage casing – maybe 10 feet in case
   you break a few sausages)

1. Finely grind the turkey and the fatback. Mix well.
2. Sweat the onions in butter with a sprig of thyme and a bay leaf.
3. Mix together the ground turkey and fatback with the onions, milk, truffles, a pinch of
nutmeg, and salt and pepper to taste. Mix in the egg whites one at a time.
4. Place the forcemeat in a pastry bag fitted with a ¾ inch plain pastry nozzle. Slip one
end of the casing over the nozzle and tie the other end. Gently squeeze the forcemeat into
the casing. You will have one long sausage that you can then divide into links by tying a
piece of string every 5 inches. Prick each sausage with a needle.
5. Cook the sausages in simmering water for about 15 minutes. Do not bring to a full boil.
6. Broil or sauté before serving. Garnish with sautéed apple slices.

Wine notes
Either red or white is fine with these sausages since they are rather mild. I'd have a Sancerre or a Fumé Blanc for white, a Gamay for red.

Meats

Tournedos d'Agneau, Sauce Chevreuil

Roasted Lamb Loin with a Pepper and Vinegar Sauce

Serves 4

1 lamb loin, trimmed
1 pound unsalted fatback
1 teaspoon olive oil
6 sprigs thyme
1 cup poivrade sauce (see page 92)
1 tablespoon red wine vinegar
2 ounces unsalted butter

1. Bone the loin and trim it of all excess fat (or have your butcher do it).
2. Slice the fatback into very thin slices. Salt and pepper the loin. Wrap the slices of fatback around the meat. Tie it every inch or so with pieces of string.
3. Put a teaspoon of olive oil in a skillet. When hot, put in the lamb and brown it on all sides. Sprinkle the lamb with the thyme leaves and cook it in the oven for 12 minutes at 400 degrees. Remove lamb from the pan and keep warm.
4. Discard the remaining fat from the skillet and deglaze with vinegar. Reduce. Add the poivrade sauce. Bring to a boil and check for salt and pepper. Remove from heat and whisk in the butter. Set aside.
5. Cut the lamb loin into slices ½ inch thick. Arrange lamb on a plate and strain the sauce around it.
6. Sprinkle thyme flowers on top. Garnish with a ratatouille niçoise (see page 183).

This preparation offers intense flavors. The poivrade sauce is one of my favorite sauces; of course, it's the usual companion to venison, but lamb is also a perfect match. As you can tell by this recipe, I like my lamb rare. You can increase the cooking time by 5 minutes for medium rare.

Wine notes

It's a mega-sauce, but it should be easy to match with a California Cabernet, huge in flavor with a high concentration on the tannic side.

Noisettes d'Agneau au Romarin

Sautéed Lamb Loin with Rosemary

Serves 4

2 pound lamb loin, trimmed
2 anchovy filets
2 ounces unsalted butter
1 tablespoon olive oil
3 shallots, chopped
2 tablespoons tarragon vinegar
2 tablespoons demi-glace (see page 83)
4 sprigs rosemary

1. Trim all excess fat and sinew from the loin. Cut the lamb into 1¼ inch thick slices (noisettes). Tie a piece of string around each noisette so it will keep its shape while cooking.
2. Mash together the anchovies and the butter to make a paste. Set aside.
3. Sauté the noisettes in olive oil for about 4 minutes on each side. Do not overcook. Remove the noisettes from the pan and keep warm between two plates.
4. Discard the fat left in the pan and add the shallots. Sauté for one minute, then deglaze with tarragon vinegar. Reduce by one half. Add demi-glace. Reduce again by one half. Remove from heat and whip in the anchovy butter, a small amount at a time. Salt and pepper to taste. Keep the sauce warm but do not boil. Add the sprigs of rosemary. Let the sauce sit for 2 minutes to pick up the rosemary flavor.
5. Place the noisettes on a warm platter. Remove the rosemary sprigs from the sauce and place them on top of the meat. Pour the sauce around the lamb. Garnish with small grilled or roasted peppers (see page 182) and baked eggplant (see page 182).

Lamb and rosemary – they were made for each other. The anchovies in this dish are a touch from the Southwest of France; they use a lot of anchovies in their cooking, especially around Biarritz.

Wine notes
Because of its southwestern influence, I would have a Pauillac with this lamb.

Tournedos d'Agneau aux Lentilles Rouges

Filet Mignon of Lamb with Red Wine Sauce and Lentils

Serves 4

12 three-ounce lamb noisettes (slices of lamb loin, about 1¼ inches thick)
¼ pound dried lentils
1 carrot, finely diced
1 stalk celery, finely diced
8 pearl onions
1 clove garlic, crushed
1 bouquet garni
2 cups red wine
1 pinch nutmeg
1 teaspoon olive oil
1 tablespoon balsamic vinegar
½ cup poivrade sauce (see page 92)
2 ounces unsalted butter
1 tablespoon chopped scallion

1. Soak lentils in cold water for a couple of hours. Drain and rinse. Put them into a pot with a mirepoix (fine dice) of carrot and celery. Add pearl onions, garlic, bouquet garni, red wine, and nutmeg. Cover and cook slowly until the lentils are soft. Add salt and pepper at the end.
2. Salt and pepper the noisettes. Sauté them in a little olive oil over high heat for 4 minutes on each side. Remove lamb from the pan and keep warm. Discard the fat left over in the pan. Deglaze with the vinegar. Add the poivrade sauce. Let cook for a minute, then remove from heat and whip in the butter. Rectify the seasoning.
3. Place the noisettes on a plate and pour the sauce over them. Garnish with the previously buttered lentils. Sprinkle chopped scallions on the lentils.

Lentils seem to have fallen from people's taste, but I think they are wonderful hot or cold (with chopped onions and a vinaigrette). Lentils are one of the oldest legumes known to man. They go very well with lamb.

Wine notes
Here again we have very intense flavors in the sauce. A big California Cabernet Sauvignon is a must, or have a St. Julien for a switch.

Filet de Porc aux Abricots

Pork Tenderloin with Apricots

Serves 4

2 pork tenderloins
1 dozen sun-dried apricots
2 cups red wine
10 ounces raisins
2 tablespoons honey
½ teaspoon crushed cumin
½ teaspoon chopped dill
½ teaspoon chopped mint
½ teaspoon crushed peppercorns
1 tablespoon olive oil
¼ cup red wine vinegar
2 shallots, finely chopped
½ cup chicken stock

1. The day before you intend to prepare the pork, soak the apricots in water. Make a marinade by mixing together the red wine, honey, raisins, cumin, dill, mint, and peppercorns. Place the pork tenderloins in the marinade; refrigerate overnight.
2. Take the tenderloins out of the marinade and pat dry. Save the marinade. Cut the meat into pieces 2 inches thick, then flatten them with the palm of your hand. Salt and pepper the meat.
3. Put the olive oil in a skillet. Add the pork slices and sauté over high heat for 3 minutes on each side. Remove the pork from the skillet and set aside.
4. Discard the excess fat from the pan and deglaze with vinegar. Add the shallots and reduce the liquid until almost dry. Add the chicken broth and the marinade. Bring sauce to a boil. Reduce for 5 minutes over low heat. Add the pork and the apricots. Simmer for 15 minutes.
5. Serve with a turnip purée or with a rutabaga purée. (Prepare exactly as you would mashed potatoes.)

This is an adaptation of a very old Roman recipe attributed to Apicius. I like pork, and this is a nice, different way of cooking it.

Wine notes
A red Côte-du-Rhône, like a Gigondas or a Cornas, will be nice.

Filet de Boeuf aux Echalotes

Tenderloin of Beef Sautéed with Vinegar and Shallots

Serves 4

2 pounds trimmed tenderloin of beef
2 tablespoons red wine vinegar
½ cup demi-glace (see page 83)
2 tablespoons heavy cream
2 ounches unsalted butter
6 shallots, chopped

1. Cut the tenderloin into 8 even slices. Salt and pepper the slices.
2. Using a large enough sauté pan, put a tablespoon of butter in the pan. When hot, put in the tenderloin and cook quickly for 2 minutes on each side. Remove meat from pan and keep warm between two plates.
3. Discard the cooking butter and deglaze the pan with the vinegar. Reduce. Add the demi-glace and cream. Bring to a boil; let reduce for 2 minutes. Whip in the butter. Do not boil. Add the shallots. Pour the juice that has bled from the tenderloin into the sauce. Stir and taste for seasoning.
4. Pour the sauce over the tenderloins. Garnish with potato-leek pancakes (see page 190).

A piece of prime beef is a delight. This recipe will show you a simple but different dish with lots of taste.

Wine notes
This is the perfect dish for one of those big California Cabernets. The sauce in this dish can handle any of them. Maybe you are lucky and have some 74's left in your cellar.

Mignon de Veau au Sauternes

Veal Scaloppini Cooked with Sauternes

Serves 4

2 pounds trimmed veal tenderloin
6 ounces wild mushrooms (cèpes, chanterelles, or shiitake)
4 shallots, chopped
3 ounces Sauternes
½ cup demi-glace (see page 83)
juice of ½ lemon
1 ounce unsalted butter

1. Cut the tenderloin of veal into slices 1½ inches thick. (If tenderloin is not available, use the eye of the round and cut it thinner.) Pound lightly.
2. Clean the wild mushrooms and sauté them quickly in a little olive oil. Add one teaspoon chopped shallots, and salt and pepper to taste. Keep warm.
3. Salt and pepper the veal. Sauté in hot butter for 4 minutes on each side. Make sure the pan is very hot; otherwise, the veal will boil in its juices and become tough.
4. Remove the veal from the pan and discard the excess fat. Add the remaining shallots and sauté for a minute. Deglaze with the Sauternes. Add the demi-glace and reduce. Add lemon juice. Whisk in the butter. Put veal back in the pan and simmer for a minute or two.
5. Place the veal on one side of a plate, the mushrooms on the other side. Spoon the sauce over the veal and sprinkle chopped chives over the mushrooms. Garnish with fresh pasta.

A different veal, very simple and tasty. The shiitake mushroom is very good in this preparation and is also readily available.

When deglazing a pan, always discard the leftover fat. I even lightly wipe the pan.

Wine notes
A toss-up between white and red. I might have a light Margaux with this veal. If white, most likely a Hermitage or a dry Sauvignon from the Sonoma county.

Tournedos de Veau, Sauce Ciboulette

Veal with a Watercress and Chive Sauce

Serves 4

4 pieces of veal (top round), 6 ounces each and cut ¾ inch thick
1 carrot
1 stalk celery
5 shallots
4 mushroom caps
1 sprig thyme
¼ cup dry white wine
¼ cup chicken stock
¼ cup heavy cream
1 bunch watercress
2 tablespoons chopped chives
1 tablespoon unsalted butter
juice of ½ lemon
2 ounces Madeira

1. Cut the veal as for a cordon bleu. Slit it laterally across the center like a billfold to make a pocket.
2. Cut a fine mirepoix (small dice) of carrots, celery, 3 shallots, and mushrooms. In melted butter, first sweat the carrots. Keep the heat low so that the vegetables will not brown. Then sweat the celery, shallots, and mushrooms. Add salt, pepper, and thyme. Set aside to cool.
3. Salt and pepper the veal. Stuff with the mirepoix.
4. In a non-corrosive pan, make a reduction of white wine and 2 chopped shallots. (Reduce liquid until almost dry.) Put wine reduction in a bowl and set aside.
5. Using the same pan, combine the chicken broth and heavy cream. Reduce by half and set aside.
6. Drop the watercress and chives into boiling water for 1 minute. In the blender, purée the blanched watercress and chives together. Add the butter, the wine reduction, and the stock and cream reduction to the purée in the blender. Mix well. Add the lemon juice and salt and pepper to taste. Mix again. Keep the sauce hot in a bain-marie. Do not let the sauce boil.
7. Sauté the tournedos in butter for about 7 minutes on each side over medium heat. Remove tournedos from the pan and discard the fat.
8. Deglaze the pan with Madeira, then pour the Madeira over the tournedos. Pour the watercress and chive sauce around the meat. Serve at once.

Apart from being a very colourful dish, this is a very nice way to cook veal because the veal stays very moist and the flavor of the vegetables goes right through the meat. The sauce is very simple and has a little bite to it from the watercress. It's a great combination.

Wine notes
A Cabernet Sauvignon on the soft side is well suited to this dish. A Merlot is all right too. I think a white wine would not show too well because of the watercress.

Mignon de Veau à l'Oseille

Sautéed Veal with Sorrel and Orange Sauce

Serves 4

24 to 32 ounces top-round veal, trimmed and cut into slices 1 inch thick and 3 inches wide
½ pound mushrooms, sliced
½ ounce chopped truffle (if available)
1 teaspoon chopped chervil
12 ounces sorrel leaves
2 ounces unsalted butter
2 tablespoons heavy cream
1 orange
2 ounces dry white wine
½ cup demi-glace (see page 83)

1. Quickly sauté the sliced mushrooms and chopped truffle (if used) in a little butter for 2 or 3 minutes. Salt and pepper. Add the chervil and keep warm.
2. Chop the sorrel coarsely. Put it in a small pan with a teaspoon of butter. Cook for 2 minutes over high heat. Add the cream, and salt and pepper to taste. Bring to a boil, then remove from heat and keep warm.
3. Peel the orange and cut the skin into very fine julienne. Blanch the julienne in boiling water for one minute.
4. Put a little butter in a fairly large sauté pan. Sauté the veal over high heat for 3 minutes on each side. (Make sure that the pan is very hot, so that the veal does not boil and become tough.) Remove from pan and keep warm.
5. Discard the extra fat left in the sauté pan and add white wine. Reduce. Put in the orange zest and the demi-glace. Bring to a boil. Add the mushrooms, salt and pepper to taste, and a few drops of orange juice.
6. Spoon the sorrel and cream combination onto a platter. Place the pieces of veal on top, and pour the sauce around.
7. Serve with fresh pasta and a tomato fondue (see page 96) on the side.

The sorrel and the orange zest combine to create an exciting taste, sharp but smooth.

Wine notes
Drink a red wine with a sophisticated taste – a Côte de Nuits, perhaps. For a white wine, my choice would be a Chardonnay, very rich, luscious, and oaky.

Ris de Veau en Chemises

Sweetbreads Braised in Cabbage Leaves

Serves 4

2 pounds sweetbreads
1 carrot, sliced
1 leek (white part only), sliced
1 stalk celery, sliced
1 bouquet garni
6 peppercorns
8 cabbage leaves, blanched
1 teaspoon unsalted butter
8 mushrooms, diced
2 shallots, chopped
4 ounces port
½ cup chicken stock (see page 82)
½ cup heavy cream
1 ounce truffle juice (if available)
16 tiny carrot balls, boiled (for garnish)
16 tiny turnip balls, boiled (for garnish)

1. Soak the sweetbreads under cold, running water for 2 to 3 hours.
2. Make a court bouillon using 2 quarts water, sliced carrot, leek, celery, the bouquet garni, salt, and peppercorns. Boil gently until the vegetables are soft. Add the sweetbreads and bring the court bouillon to a boil. Remove from heat and let the sweetbreads cool off in the court bouillon.
3. Clean and trim the sweetbreads. Remove all fat and sinews. Cut the sweetbreads into pieces the size of an egg. Wrap each piece in the previously blanched cabbage leaves. (Blanch the cabbage leaves by dropping them into boiling water for 2 minutes.)
4. Put the butter in a shallow skillet. Add the shallots and mushrooms. Stir for 3 to 4 minutes over low heat.
5. Place the wrapped sweetbreads on top of the shallots and mushrooms. Add the port, chicken stock, cream, and truffle juice. Bring to a boil. Cover the pot and braise for 10 minutes in the oven at 300 degrees.
6. Remove the wrapped sweetbreads from the pan and keep warm.
7. Reduce the sauce and season with salt and pepper. Arrange the sweetbreads on a plate and pour the sauce over them.
8. Garnish with carrot and turnip balls previously scooped, boiled, and sautéed in butter.

An involved preparation, but if you want to show off to your special guests, this is the dish to make. Buy nice, large, white sweetbreads. Make sure to use large enough cabbage leaves so the sweetbreads will be well wrapped.

Wine notes
A Margaux or a light Cabernet Sauvignon for red; a Graves or a Sauvignon Blanc for white.

Ris de Veau au Vermouth

Sautéed Sweetbreads with Vermouth, Cream, and Cucumbers

Serves 4

2 pounds sweetbreads
1 carrot, sliced
1 onion, sliced
1 bouquet garni
2 cloves
6 peppercorns
2 ounces unsalted butter
2 leeks (white part only), sliced
½ pound mushrooms, sliced
3 shallots, chopped
2 ounces dry vermouth
1 cup heavy cream
1 teaspoon chopped chervil
1 large cucumber, peeled and turned (see step 8)

1. Put the sweetbreads in a bowl. Soak under cold, running water for 2 or 3 hours.
2. Drain sweetbreads and put them in a pot. Cover with cold water. Add sliced carrot, sliced onion, bouquet garni, cloves, and peppercorns. Bring to a boil and remove pot from the heat.
3. Let sweetbreads sit in the poaching liquid until cold. Take them out of the liquid. Peel the sweetbreads and cut them in half.
4. Melt a teaspoon butter in a small pan. Add the leeks and cover the pan. Cook slowly for 10 minutes, and then set aside.
5. Sauté the sliced mushrooms in butter. Set aside.
6. Put a tablespoon of butter in a large sauté pan. When hot, place the sweetbreads in the pan. When the sweetbreads are lightly brown on one side, turn over and cook the other side. Set the sweetbreads to one side of the pan and add the shallots. Cook for a minute, then deglaze the pan with vermouth. (Do not remove the sweetbreads and shallots for deglazing.) Reduce the liquid. Add cream, leeks, mushrooms, salt and pepper to taste. Cook quickly until the sauce starts to thicken.
7. Put the sweetbreads in a warm dish. Sprinkle with chervil. Place the previously cooked cucumber around the sweetbreads.
8. To turn the cucumbers, first cut them in half lengthwise and remove the seeds. Cut the cucumber halves into 2 inch long pieces. Cut each of those pieces in half again. Using a small knife, turn the pieces into ovals the size and shape of large olives. Blanch the turned cucumber in boiling water for 3 minutes. Sauté the cucumber in a small pan with 1 teaspoon of butter and 1 teaspoon of sugar. Let the cucumber get brown but not too dark. Place around the sweetbreads.
9. Serve fresh pasta on the side.

Nice combination, dry vermouth and sweetbreads. A very pleasing dish, easy to execute and not too time-consuming. The sweetbreads can be cooked a day ahead.

Wine notes
Here again, I would go with a lighter Cabernet Sauvignon for red or a Sauvignon Blanc for white.

Blanquette de Ris de Veau
Sweetbreads Stewed with Vegetables and Turkey Sausage

Serves 4

2 pounds sweetbreads
2 artichokes
1 cup dry white wine
5 large carrots
1 small bunch celery
1 large onion, sliced
1 leek (white part only), sliced
1 bouquet garni
6 peppercorns
12 pearl onions
12 button mushrooms
1 teaspoon unsalted butter
½ tablespoon beurre manié (made by mixing equal parts of softened butter and flour in a bowl)
2 egg yolks
½ cup heavy cream
juice of ½ lemon
4 boudins blancs (see page 166)

1. Soak the sweetbreads under cold running water for 2 to 3 hours.
2. Boil the artichokes in salted water for 25 minutes. Remove from water and let cool. When cool, remove leaves and chokes. Cut artichoke bottoms into quarters. Set aside.
3. In a large pot, make a court bouillon by putting together the white wine, 1 sliced carrot, 2 sliced celery stalks, the sliced onion, and sliced leek. Add the bouquet garni, a little salt, a few peppercorns, and a quart of water. Bring to a boil and let the court bouillon boil gently for 15 minutes. Add the sweetbreads and simmer for 10 minutes. Remove the pot from the heat and let it stand to cool.
4. Turn the remaining carrots into pieces the size and shape of an olive. Do the same with the remaining celery. Cook them in boiling water until done but still crisp. Set aside.
5. Cook the pearl onions in boiling water until done but still crisp. Set aside.
6. Cook the mushrooms in a small amount of water with a teaspoon of butter and a splash of lemon juice. Set aside.
7. Remove the sweetbreads from the cooled court bouillon. Set them aside. Strain the broth and reserve a couple tablespoons of it. Return the rest of the broth to the heat and boil until it is reduced by half. Whisk in the beurre manié, a bit at a time. Simmer for a minute or two to thicken.
8. In a bowl, make a liaison by whipping the egg yolks, cream, and lemon juice together.
9. Remove the thickened bouillon from the heat and stir in the liaison.
10. Peel and devein the sweetbreads. Cut them in slices ½ inch thick. Cut the boudins blancs in the same way.
11. Put a tablespoon or two of the reserved broth in a shallow pan. Add all the vegetables and meats. Cover the pan and slowly warm everything. When hot, pour in the sauce. Let all the ingredients stew for a while, but do not let the sauce boil.
12. Serve with fresh pasta.

From a very classic base, *blanquette de veau,* to a new flavor with sweetbreads and turkey sausages. An interesting combination, very flavorful and mellow.

Wine notes
I would go with a white wine – a premium Chardonnay, buttery and rich. Don't serve it too cold or it will clash with this dish.

Rognons de Veau au Calvados

Veal Kidneys with Calvados, Mustard, and Cream

Serves 2

2 veal kidneys
1 tablespoon unsalted butter
1 tablespoon peanut oil
1 tablespoon chopped shallots
4 ounces Calvados (if unavailable, use brandy)
¼ cup heavy cream
1 teaspoon Dijon mustard
1 pinch chopped chervil

1. Cut the kidneys first in half, then in slices about ¼ inch thick.
2. Put the butter and oil in a pan and sauté the kidneys very fast for about 4 minutes. Remove the kidneys from the pan and set in a strainer.
3. Add the shallots and Calvados to the pan. Do not flame. Add heavy cream and reduce by one half. Add the Dijon mustard.
4. Put the kidneys back into the sauce and bring to a fast boil.
5. Serve right away. Garnish with chopped chervil.

If you like kidneys, you will want to keep them rare. Substitute brandy if you don't have a bottle of Calvados at hand.

Wine notes
With the kidneys I would probably have a Pinot Noir or maybe a Merlot.

Vegetables
and
Garnishes

Poivrons Grillés

Grilled Peppers

1 whole Bell pepper per person
olive oil

1. Place the whole peppers in a roasting pan. Brush them with olive oil. Roast at 400 degrees until the skins start to peel off (about 5 to 8 minutes). Remove pan from oven. Rub the peppers with a towel to remove all of the skin.
2. Cut the peppers in half and remove the seeds.
3. Dip the halved peppers into olive oil. Place them on a hot grill. Cook for 3 to 4 minutes, turning occasionally.

Aubergines au Four

Baked Eggplant

Serves 6

6 very small eggplants (4 to 5 inches long)
4 cloves garlic
½ cup olive oil
2 tablespoons herbes de Provence (available at a gourmet store)
2 tablespoons chopped parsley

1. Marinate the garlic cloves in olive oil for 10 minutes. Remove the garlic and cut 2 cloves into thin slivers. Mix the oil with the herbes de Provence, salt, and pepper.
2. Cut a few slits in each eggplant. Insert a garlic sliver in each slit. Brush the eggplants with seasoned oil. Wrap each one in aluminum foil.
3. Bake the eggplants at 400 degrees for about 30 minutes. (Cooking time will depend on the size of the eggplants.)
4. Take the eggplants out of the foil. Slit each one lengthwise. Spoon a teaspoon of seasoned oil over each. Chop the remaining 2 cloves of garlic and mix with the parsley. Sprinkle on each eggplant.

Ratatouille Niçoise

Serves 4

1 medium eggplant
2 medium zucchini
2 green peppers
2 large tomatoes, peeled and seeded
3 tablespoons olive oil
1 onion, sliced
3 cloves garlic, finely chopped
1 bouquet garni (3 sprigs each of thyme, basil, rosemary, lavender, savoury, and sage)

1. Peel the eggplant and the zucchini. Cut into ½ inch cubes. Cut the peppers in half and remove the seeds. Slice the peppers. Coarsely chop up the peeled and seeded tomatoes.
2. Put 1 tablespoon olive oil in a skillet. When hot, add the zucchini. Sauté until golden brown. Remove the zucchini from the pan and place in a kettle or deeper pan. Repeat this procedure with all the vegetables, sautéeing them one at a time. Do not overcook. Add olive oil as needed.
3. When all the vegetables have been sautéed and placed in the kettle, add the chopped garlic and the bouquet garni. Cook slowly for half an hour, or until the vegetables are tender. Serve with chopped parsley on top.

Gâteau d'Epinards

Spinach Custard

Serves 4

6 ounces fresh spinach
2 large eggs
½ cup milk
½ cup heavy cream
2 tablespoons unsalted butter
2 to 3 gratings nutmeg

1. Thoroughly wash spinach and remove stems.
2. Bring salted water to a boil. Drop in the spinach and cook for 1 minute. Drain the spinach and cool it off.
3. Put the eggs, milk, cream, 2 or 3 gratings of nutmeg, and salt and pepper to taste in a bowl. Mix well and set aside.
4. Melt 1½ tablespoons of butter in a skillet. Add the spinach and cook over low heat for about 5 minutes. Add the sautéed spinach to the custard mixture.
5. Butter the bottom and sides of a custard mold. Pour in the spinach mixture. Set the mold in a roasting pan filled ¾ of the way with hot water. Bake at 350 degrees for about 40 minutes.

Everyone will love spinach cooked this way. You could almost make a meal of it.

Flan de Maïs

Corn Custard

Serves 6

1 cup cooked corn kernels (if fresh not available, use canned corn)
1 tablespoon chopped onions
2 eggs
½ cup heavy cream
1 pinch nutmeg
1 pinch cayenne pepper
1 teaspoon chopped parsley
1 teaspoon unsalted butter

1. Sauté the onions in butter until cooked. Set aside.
2. In a bowl, place the eggs, cream, nutmeg, cayenne, and salt and pepper to taste. Mix well. Add the corn and parsley.
3. Pour the mixture into small, buttered ramekins. Place the ramekins into a shallow pan filled with water (a bain-marie). Bake at 350 degrees until firm (approximately 15 minutes).

This corn custard is very nice with game birds or fowl.

Gâteau de Courgettes

Zucchini and Leek Custard

Serves 8

3 medium zucchini
6 cups water
½ pound leeks (white part only), sliced
2 eggs
1 egg white
5 tablespoons heavy cream
1 pinch grated nutmeg

1. Trim the ends from the zucchini. Cut each zucchini crosswise into 4 pieces.
2. Bring water to a boil. Add the cut-up leeks and cook for 10 minutes. Add zucchini and continue boiling until tender. Drain and press vegetables to extract all water.
3. Put the zucchini and leek mixture in the blender. Run until smooth.
4. Place mixture in a bowl. Add the eggs, egg white, cream, nutmeg, salt and pepper to taste. Mix well. Pour mixture into buttered ramekins. Set the ramekins in a bain-marie. Cook in the oven at medium heat (350 degrees) for about 45 minutes.

A great marriage. The leeks add so much to the zucchini purée. This dish is especially good with veal or chicken.

Croquettes d'Ail

Garlic Fritters

Serves 6

20 cloves garlic, unpeeled
6 large hardboiled eggs (yolks only)
1¾ ounces unsalted butter, softened
1 teaspoon chopped basil
2 tablespoons flour
egg wash (beat together 1 egg, 1 tsp. water, 1 tsp. oil)
3½ ounces fresh bread crumbs

1. Blanch the garlic in boiling water. Drain and blanch the garlic a second time in fresh boiling water.
2. Peel the garlic cloves and purée them in the blender. Add the hardboiled egg yolks, soft butter, chopped basil, and salt and pepper to taste to the garlic purée. Mix again.
3. Shape the mixture into tiny balls (the size and shape of garlic cloves) and freeze them.
4. When frozen, roll the balls first in the flour and then in the egg wash. Then roll them in the fresh bread crumbs.
5. If you have an electric fryolator, set it at 325 degrees. When oil becomes hot, drop in fritters (a few at a time) and fry until golden brown. Before removing all the fritters, break one in half to make sure it's warm inside.
6. If you do not have an electric fryolater, use a deep skillet filled with 2 inches of oil. When the oil reaches 325 degrees (use your thermometer), follow the same procedures as above.

The temperature is critical for these fritters. If the oil is too hot, the fritters will burn before they cook inside. If the oil is too cold, the fritters will fall apart.

These garlic fritters are a perfect garnish for rack of lamb.

Beignets de Pommes

Apple Fritters

Serves 6

5 ounces flour
2 eggs
1½ tablespoons olive oil
½ teaspoon salt
3⅓ ounces beer
3 apples

1. Place 4½ ounces of flour, the eggs, oil, and salt in a bowl. Mix well. Add the beer and mix again. Refrigerate for 2 to 3 hours before using.
2. Peel the apples and slice them ½ inch thick.
3. Dredge the apple slices in the remaining flour, then dip them in the batter. Deep fry the slices at 350 degrees for 4 to 5 minutes. They should be soft inside and golden brown outside. Drain on a paper towel.

As the recipe stands, the apple fritters make a good garnish for game birds and especially for confit. For a fun dessert, marinate the apple slices for 15 minutes in 3 ounces of Calvados and 2 tablespoons of sugar. Then proceed as above. Sprinkle the beignets with powdered sugar or cinnamon sugar.

Tourte aux Poireaux

Mushroom and Leek Pie

Serves 6

6 medium leeks, white part only
4 ounces unsalted butter
⅔ cup heavy cream
1 pinch nutmeg
4 shallots, chopped
½ pound mushrooms, sliced
1 pound puff pastry (frozen is fine)
1 egg, beaten

1. Wash the leeks carefully in cold water. Cut in half lengthwise, then slice thinly crosswise.
2. In a heavy saucepan, melt 1 ounce butter. Add the leeks. Cook slowly for 3 to 4 minutes, stirring frequently. Add another ounce butter and ¼ cup water. Cover and cook for 15 minutes over low heat. Take cover off pan and let liquid evaporate all the way. Set aside.
3. Pour heavy cream into a saucepan. Bring to a boil and reduce by half. Pour reduced cream over the leeks. Add salt, pepper, and nutmeg to taste. Set aside to cool.
4. In a skillet, melt the remaining 2 ounces of butter. Add the shallots and sauté for a minute. Add the mushrooms and sauté until cooked. Drain and set aside to cool.
5. Roll out the pastry to ⅛ inch thick. Using a 10 inch plate, cut out a circle. Using a 12 inch plate, cut out a second circle of dough.
6. Lay the smaller circle on a sheet pan. Cover it to within one inch of the edge with the leeks. Spread the mushrooms over the leeks. Put the 12 inch cover on top. Seal the edge with egg wash (1 beaten egg). Cut a hole in the center of the pastry cover. Brush the top with egg wash. Cook in a 375 degree oven for 15 minutes.

Make individual pies and have a great lunch, or use the tourte as a garnish to almost any dish, especially fish dishes.

Crêpes aux Poireaux et Pommes de Terre

Potato-Leek Pancakes

Serves 6

4 leeks (white part only), trimmed, cleaned, and split
3 tablespoons unsalted butter
½ cup heavy cream
2 pounds potatoes, peeled
1 pinch nutmeg
3 tablespoons peanut oil

1. Cut the leeks into thin slices. Melt 2 tablespoons butter in a heavy skillet or pan. Add the leeks and cook for 2 minutes, stirring. Cover the pan and cook for 15 to 20 minutes over low heat. Do not brown.

2. Add the cream and nutmeg to the pan and bring to a boil. Simmer until it thickens. Season with salt and pepper. Set aside.

3. Cut the peeled potatoes into fine julienne. You can use a mandolin or a food processor with a julienne blade. If neither of these tools is available, just grate the potatoes coarsely.

4. Rinse the potatoes under running water to get rid of the starch. Drain, and then dry in a towel. Make sure the potatoes are really dry.

5. In a heavy-bottomed skillet, put 2 tablespoons of oil. When hot, place half of the potatoes in the pan; spread them around like a pancake. Sprinkle with a little salt and pepper. Cover with the leek and cream mixture, then top with the rest of the potatoes. Dust lightly with salt and pepper. Cover the pan and cook for 10 to 12 minutes on medium heat. Shake the pan frequently so the potatoes don't stick.

6. Flip the pancakes over and out of the pan, or turn the pan over so that the pancake rests on the lid. Add 1 tablespoon oil and 1 tablespoon butter to the empty pan. When hot, slide the pancake back into the pan, cooked side up. Cook for 10 to 15 minutes over low heat, until the potatoes are cooked and tender.

7. Slide the pancake onto a serving dish. Sprinkle with chopped parsley or a touch of thyme leaves. Serve at once.

Risotto de Riz Sauvage

Wild Rice Risotto

Serves 6

1 cup wild rice
3 cups chicken stock (see page 82, or use water)
1 småll bouquet garni
8 ounces bacon, cut in small strips
1 onion, chopped
4 mushroom caps, diced ¼ inch square
1 tomato, peeled, seeded, and chopped

1. Rinse wild rice under running water. Place the rice in a pot. Add 2½ cups chicken broth (if not available, use water). Add the bouquet garni. Bring to a boil and cover the pot. Simmer until the rice becomes fluffy.
2. Place the bacon in a skillet. When the fat starts to melt, add the onions. Cook for a few minutes, then add the mushrooms. Sauté for 2 more minutes. Drain in a colander to get rid of the excess fat.
3. Put the rice in a skillet or baking dish. Add the bacon, onion, mushroom combination. Add the chopped tomato, freshly ground pepper, a little salt, and the remaining ½ cup of chicken stock. Cover the skillet or baking dish with foil. Cook the rice in the oven at 300 degrees until all the liquid has been absorbed. Check the rice every five minutes or so.

Ravioli

1½ cups plus 3 tablespoons flour
2 large eggs
2 teaspoons milk
1 teaspoon salt
1 egg, beaten for egg wash
cornmeal (to cover tray)

1. Put flour in bowl of food processor. Add eggs, milk, and salt. Blend until dough becomes dry enough and does not stick to the sides of the bowl. Add a little more flour if necessary. Take the dough out of the bowl. Shape it into a ball and wrap it in plastic wrap. Refrigerate for at least half an hour.
2. Divide the pasta dough in half. Roll it out on a floured pastry board. Make sure that the pasta is very thin and even. Using a pasta machine will make this operation much simpler.
3. When the first sheet is rolled out, place it on a flat, floured surface. Brush it all over with egg wash. For miniature ravioli ½ inch square, arrange ½ teaspoonfuls of filling symmetrically over the surface of the pasta.
4. Roll out the second ball of pasta dough to same thickness as the first. Carefully cover the filling-dotted pasta with the second layer of dough. Using a ruler or a stick, carefully press crosswise between the portions of filling. Then press lengthwise, applying enough pressure to make a good seal.
5. Evenly cut out the ravioli with a ravioli cutter. Arrange the ravioli on a tray dusted with cornmeal. Let stand for 20 minutes.
6. Bring 6 quarts of salted water to a boil. Drop in the ravioli. Return to the boil and cook the ravioli for 3 more minutes.

This is a basic recipe for ravioli. You can fill the ravioli with almost anything you wish. One possibility is tomato fondue (see page 96) flavored with basil purée, corn kernels, or finely chopped anchovies. You can also use a mixture of chopped spinach and puréed mushrooms. (Before you chop the spinach, blanch it in boiling water and sauté it in butter; before you purée the mushrooms, sauté them with butter and shallots.)

Crêpes

Serves 12

2½ ounces flour
1 egg
1 egg yolk
1 cup milk
2 tablespoons unsalted butter
4 tablespoons oil

1. In a bowl, mix the flour, egg, egg yolk, and oil with a whisk until all ingredients are well incorporated. Add the milk and mix some more. Add salt to taste.
2. Add vegetables, flavorings, etc. (See corn and spinach crêpes below.) Refrigerate batter for an hour.
3. Cook in crêpes pan with a little butter for about 3 minutes on each side. (The crêpes should be the size of a silver dollar piece.)

Crêpes au Maïs et Epinards
Corn and Spinach Fritters

Crêpe batter
4½ ounces canned corn
1 package frozen spinach (or one cup cooked
   fresh spinach)
1 pinch nutmeg

1. Prepare crêpes batter (see above).
2. Cook spinach in boiling water. Drain, squeeze, and chop coarsely.
3. Incorporate the chopped spinach, drained corn, nutmeg, salt, and pepper into the batter.
4. Refrigerate and prepare as described above.

Desserts

Poires Pochées au Vin Rouge

Pears Poached in Red Wine and Raspberries

Serves 6

6 pears (whole, with stems intact)
1 pint raspberries
juice of 1 lemon
½ cup sugar
1 bottle red wine (a Côte du Rhône is preferred)
4 tablespoons honey
2 cloves
6 peppercorns

1. In the blender, put the raspberries, lemon juice, and half of the sugar. Run until puréed. Strain through a sieve to remove the seeds.
2. Place the purée in a saucepan (not aluminum). Add red wine, the rest of the sugar, honey, cloves, and peppercorns. Bring to a boil and simmer for 10 minutes.
3. Carefully peel the pears with a vegetable peeler. (Leave them whole with the stems on.) Poach them in the red wine for about 20 to 30 minutes at low heat.
4. When pears are cooked, remove and set aside in a bowl. Reduce poaching liquid by half. Pour over pears. Chill before serving.

Make sure you choose ripe pears. This is a wonderful dessert, very refreshing in the summer.

Wine notes
A glass of Sauternes would be perfect with the fruit flavors.

Pêches Pochées au Sauternes

Peaches Poached in Sauternes, Served with a Strawberry Sauce

Serves 4

4 whole, ripe peaches
2 cups Sauternes
1 vanilla bean
simple syrup (you can buy light syrup at any grocery store)
1 cup strawberries
5 ounces sugar
1 cup heavy cream
juice of ½ lemon
4 mint leaves

1. Drop the peaches in boiling water for a second and peel them as you would a tomato. Cut peaches in half and remove the pits.
2. Place the peeled, halved peaches in a sauteuse. Add the Sauternes and a vanilla bean, then add enough syrup to cover the peaches. Bring slowly to a boil and cook until the peaches are soft but not mushy. (Use a fork to test the fruit.) Remove from heat and let cool off, then set aside in refrigerator.
3. Put the strawberries through a fine sieve. Place the pulp in a bowl and add the sugar.
4. In another bowl, whip the cream just until it starts to thicken. Add the strawberry pulp and the lemon juice.
5. Serve the chilled peaches on individual plates with the strawberry sauce around them. Garnish with a mint leaf and serve a macaroon (see page 209) on the side.

Wine notes
Perfectly ripe peaches are a must for this dessert. Serve a glass of Sauternes with it.

Gratin de Fruits

Fruit Baked in Custard Sauce

Serves 4

1 apple
1 pear
1 peach
12 blueberries
8 raspberries
8 strawberries
1 teaspoon unsalted butter
2 ounces kirsch
2 tablespoons water
2 tablespoons sugar
1 cup crème anglaise (see page 219)

1. Peel the apple and the pear. Cut them into thin slices. Slice the peach. Cut the strawberries into quarters.
2. In a shallow skillet put the butter, kirsch, water, and sugar. Bring to a boil and add the apple, pear, and peach slices. Simmer for 2 to 3 minutes. Add the rest of the fruits and cook for 1 more minute.
3. Place the fruits in a small, deep, ovenproof dish. Cover them with crème anglaise. Bake briefly at 400 degrees until the top starts to get brown. Serve immediately.

Another recipe from my apprentice days, but with a little variation of the fruits. In those days we used only *fraises des bois* (wild strawberries).

Wine notes
Here again, a Sauternes will show very well with the fruits.

Tarte aux Pommes Chaude

Hot Apple Tart

Make 1 tart per person; repeat the recipe as needed.

1 medium apple (preferably Granny Smith)
½ teaspoon lemon juice
½ pound puff pastry (frozen is all right)
1 ounce unsalted butter
1 ounce sugar

1. Peel and cut the apple into thin slices. Sprinkle with a little lemon juice to keep apples from turning brown. Set aside.
2. Roll out puff pastry ¼ inch thick. Cut a circle 8 inches in diameter. Score a second circle inside the first, 1 inch from the edge. This will form a border when cooking.
3. Neatly arrange the apple slices on the pastry circle, keeping the slices inside the border rim. Put a few small pieces of butter on top and sprinkle the apples with a little sugar.
4. Bake at 375 degrees for 15 minutes. Add a little more butter and sugar; return the tart to the oven for another 10 minutes.
5. Serve hot with a Calvados-flavored crème anglaise (see page 219).

Wine notes
What a tart. Probably the simplest dessert ever created, but a thrill with a glass or two of a great Sauternes.

Tarte au Citron Vert Créole

Lime Meringue Pie, Creole Style

Serves 6

1 baked pie crust (see recipe for pâte sucrée on page 224)
3 egg yolks
1 cup sugar
2 tablespoons flour
¼ cup melted butter
¼ cup lime juice
1 tablespoon grated lemon rind
¾ cup heavy cream
1 cup sour cream

1. Put the egg yolks and sugar in a double boiler. When water boils, reduce heat to medium. Whip until the mixture becomes fluffy. Add the flour, melted butter, lime juice, and lemon rind. Mix well. Stir in the cream. Stirring constantly, cook for about 15 minutes until the mixture thickens.
2. Allow filling to cool to room temperature, then fold in the sour cream. Mix well. Pour filling into pie crust.

Meringue
3 egg whites
¼ teaspoon cream of tartar
6 tablespoons sugar
few drops vanilla

1. Prepare the meringue by whipping 3 egg whites with ¼ teaspoon cream of tartar. When the whites start to peak, add 6 tablespoons of sugar, one at a time. Add a few drops of vanilla. Keep on whipping until the whites are stiff.
2. Using a pastry bag, pipe the meringue decoratively onto the top of the pie. Bake for 15 to 20 minutes in a 325 degree oven until the meringue is light brown.
3. Serve with a crème anglaise (see page 219) laced with orange liqueur.

Charlotte aux Fraises

Strawberry Charlotte

Serves 6

2 pounds strawberries
6½ ounces water
5 tablespoons sugar
14 ladyfingers (see recipe page 208)

1. Pick the stems off the strawberries. Put the water and sugar in a pot and bring to a fast boil. Drop in the strawberries and boil very fast for 2 minutes. Drain the berries and make sure to save the syrup.
2. Put half of the berries in the blender. Do not blend for too long, as you want to find some pieces of fruit left in the purée. Leave the other half of the strawberries whole.
3. Cut the ladyfingers in half lengthwise. Soak them in the syrup one at a time.
4. Cover the bottom and sides of a charlotte mold with half of the soaked ladyfingers. Pour in ½ inch of strawberry purée; then add a layer of soaked ladyfingers, a layer of whole strawberries, and another layer of soaked ladyfingers. Repeat this operation, starting with the purée, until all ingredients are used up.
5. Refrigerate the charlotte for about 5 hours. Dip the mold into warm water for a minute and unmold onto a platter. Serve the remaining syrup on the side, or serve a crème anglaise (page 219) with chopped pistachios added to it.

A very, very light charlotte, quite different than the regular charlotte.

Wine notes
Sauternes is always perfect with fruit desserts.

Gâteau Mousse de Framboise et Cassis

Raspberry and Black Currant Mousse Cake

Serves 8

12 ounces black currants (sometimes you can buy them frozen or in jars at specialty shops)
5 ounces simple syrup (you can buy light syrup at any grocery store)
1 tablespoon powdered milk (*not* reconstituted)
1 dash vanilla
3 egg yolks
1 ounce sugar
4 leaves gelatin or 2½ teaspoons powdered gelatin, dissolved in water
3 tablespoons heavy cream
1 cup Italian meringue (see page 221)
6½ ounces crème de framboises (raspberry liqueur)
1 nine-inch pâte à biscuit (see page 207)

1. Put the currants in the mixer with 3 tablespoons syrup. Run until smooth. Put aside 2 tablespoons of the currant purée.
2. Put the remaining purée in a saucepan with the powdered milk and the vanilla. Bring to a boil and remove from heat.
3. In a bowl, whip the egg yolk and sugar until the mixture starts to form a ribbon. Pour the boiling currants over the egg yolks. Put the whole mixture into a saucepan and place the pan on the heat. Stirring constantly with a wooden spoon, cook quickly until the mixture reaches the consistency of crème anglaise.
4. Remove the pan from the heat and add 2 leaves of gelatin (previously soaked). Dissolve completely. Strain the mixture and let it cool.
5. Whip cream to a soft peak. Set aside.
6. When the custard is almost cold, add the Italian meringue. Use a whip and go slowly. Add the raspberry liqueur. Fold in the whipped cream.
7. Cut a ½ inch thick slice from the biscuit. (This will form the base for the mousse). Place the slice of biscuit in the bottom of a metal form to keep mousse from spreading. Sprinkle it with raspberry liqueur. Place the currant mousse on top of the biscuit; spread the mousse evenly. Put the cake in the freezer for a couple of hours.
8. When the mousse has set, pour the following glaçage on top: in a small pan, put 3 tablespoons of syrup, the 2 reserved tablespoons of currant purée, and 2 gelatin leaves (previously soaked). Gently warm up the glaçage and spread it on the cake.
9. Carefully remove the metal form from the cake. Serve with a raspberry coulis (see page 223).

This cake was inspired by a Charles Barrier recipe. It is a little elaborate, but worth the effort – a very pretty dessert and an intense flavor.

Gâteau de Rêves

Chocolate and Cream Cake

Serves 8

12 eggs
1¼ cup sugar
1 teaspoon vanilla
1 cup flour
5 tablespoons cocoa powder
1 pinch of salt
½ cup milk
9 ounces semi-sweet chocolate
¾ cup heavy cream

1. In a bowl, whip together 8 eggs, 1 cup sugar, and the vanilla. Place the bowl over low heat or over a pot of boiling water. Keep on whipping until the mixture has quadrupled in size (about 10 minutes). Remove from heat.
2. Sift the flour and cocoa into the egg and sugar mixture, a small amount at a time. Use a wooden spoon to fold in the flour and cocoa mixture. Add a pinch of salt.
3. When all the ingredients are well amalgamated, scoop the batter into a buttered and floured 10 inch pan.
4. Bake at 350 degrees for about 25 to 35 minutes. When baked, unmold cake onto a rack to cool.

Chocolate Mousse Filling

1. Put the milk in a small pan and add the chocolate. Melt over a bain-marie. When melted, add 4 egg yolks and 4 tablespoons of sugar. Remove from heat and stir this mixture without stopping until it has completely cooled.
2. Whip the 4 egg whites to a peak. Fold them into the cooled chocolate mixture. Refrigerate for 2 to 3 hours.
3. Whip the cream and set it in the refrigerator.
4. Reserve ⅓ of the chocolate mousse. Cut the cake into 3 equal layers. Lay the first layer on a piece of cardboard about the same size as the cake. Cover the first layer with the remaining ⅔ of the mousse. Place the second layer on top and then cover it with the chilled whipped cream. Put on the third layer. Cover the top and sides of the cake with the reserved chocolate mousse.
5. You can decorate the cake with chocolate shavings and almonds.

As the French name *gâteau de rêves* indicates, this cake really is a chocolate dream. It is one of the best chocolate desserts I have ever come across, light enough and very chocolaty.

Gâteau Chanticleer

Serves 10

12 eggs
1¼ cup sugar
1 teaspoon vanilla
1 cup flour
⅔ cup cocoa powder
1 pinch of salt
½ cup milk
9 ounces semi-sweet chocolate
1 ounce raspberry liqueur
7 tablespoons unsalted butter
4 tablespoons light corn syrup
5 ounces bitter-sweet chocolate

1. In a bowl, whip together 8 eggs, 1 cup sugar, and vanilla. Place the bowl over low heat or over a pot of boiling water. Keep on whipping until the mixture has quadrupled in size (about 10 minutes). Remove from heat.
2. Slowly sift the flour and cocoa powder into the egg and sugar mixture. Fold in the flour and cocoa with a wooden spoon. Add a pinch of salt.
3. When all ingredients are well amalgamated, scoop the batter into a buttered, floured, 10 inch pan.
4. Bake at 350 degrees for about 25 to 35 minutes. When cooked, unmold onto a rack to cool.

Chocolate Mousse Filling and Chocolate Glaze

1. Put the milk in a small pan. Add 9 ounces semi-sweet chocolate and melt it over a bain-marie. When melted, add 4 egg yolks and 4 tablespoons sugar. Remove from heat and stir the mixture without stopping until it has cooled completely.
2. Whip the 4 egg whites to a peak. Fold them into the chocolate. Refrigerate the mousse for an hour.
3. Slice the cake in half crosswise. Sprinkle the raspberry liqueur onto each half. Spread the chilled chocolate mousse between the two layers. Chill in the refrigerator until firm.
4. In a saucepan, put the butter and corn syrup. Stirring constantly over a low heat, simmer for 2 minutes. Add 5 ounces bitter-sweet chocolate and a teaspoon raspberry liqueur. Whisk until the chocolate has melted and the glaze is smooth. Let cool for a few minutes.
5. Pour and spread the glaze over the cake. Decorate the cake with fresh raspberries and chocolate leaves. Let the cake rest before serving.

Dacquoise

Serves 6

9 ounces almond powder (make by grinding whole, blanched almonds)
8 egg whites
9 ounces sugar
1 ounce corn starch
½ cup praline butter cream (mix 1 teaspoon praline paste into plain butter cream;
   see page 207)
½ cup chocolate butter cream (mix 1 tablespoon cocoa powder into plain butter cream;
   see page 207)

1. Whip the egg whites to a firm peak. Gently fold in the almond powder, sugar, and corn starch.
2. Put the mixture into a pastry bag fitted with a small nozzle the width of a pencil.
3. Butter and flour a baking sheet (or use baking parchment). Squeeze the dacquoise batter onto the baking sheet to form 3 to 4 inch circles. (You should have more than enough batter to make the 18 rounds needed for this recipe.)
4. Bake at 200 to 225 degrees until dry, about 20 to 30 minutes. Remove dacquoise from sheet and cool on a rack.
5. Take three pieces of dacquoise. Spread the bottom one with a layer of chocolate butter cream. Place another piece of dacquoise on top and spread it with a layer of praline butter cream. Put a final piece of dacquoise on top.
6. Sprinkle with powdered sugar and keep refrigerated until serving.

A truly great classical dessert. Keep the dacquoise layers dry in a tin or freeze them when completely cold.

Marjolaine

Serves 8

7 ounces whole almonds
5 ounces whole hazelnuts
10 ounces granulated sugar
1 ounce flour
8 egg whites
8 ounces crème fraîche (available at specialty stores)
12 ounces semi-sweet chocolate, melted
16 ounces heavy cream, whipped
4 ounces unsalted butter, softened
4 ounces praline paste (available at specialty stores)

1. Roast the almonds and the hazelnuts on separate trays at 400 degrees until golden brown. When the hazelnuts are roasted, rub off all their skins with a towel.
2. Grind the almonds and hazelnuts together. Add the granulated sugar and the flour to the ground nut mixture.
3. Beat the egg whites until stiff and fold them gently into the nut mixture.
4. On buttered, floured baking sheets, divide the mixture into 4 long, narrow bands (4 inches by 12 inches). Bake them at 200 to 225 degrees for about 45 minutes, or until they are brown on top but still pliable. Cool the nut meringue strips on a rack.
5. The cake will be stacked in layers with three fillings (see below). Spread half of the chocolate cream onto the first layer. Put the second layer on top and spread it with all of the plain butter cream. Put on the third layer and spread it with all of the praline butter cream. Put the last layer on top. Use the remaining chocolate cream to frost the top and sides of the cake.
6. Chill the cake in the refrigerator until firm. Just before serving, garnish with chocolate shavings and a sprinkle of confectioner's sugar.

Chocolate Cream
Mix the crème fraîche into the melted chocolate. Stirring constantly, bring the mixture to a boil. Remove from heat and let cool.

Plain butter cream (special recipe for Marjolaine)
Blend half of the whipped cream into 2 ounces of softened butter. Add the cream very slowly and gradually until the butter will not absorb any more cream.

Praline butter cream
Make another mixture of plain butter cream using the remaining whipped cream and softened butter. Blend the praline paste into the butter cream.

This is one of Fernand Point's famous desserts. I don't believe anyone can improve on Fernand Point's recipes. This is just my version of his masterpiece.

Pâte à Biscuit

Sponge Cake

Serves 6

4 egg whites
7 egg yolks
3 ounces sugar
1¼ ounces flour
1⅓ ounces potato starch (available at a specialty store)

1. Whip the egg yolks in a bowl with ¾ of the sugar until it forms a ribbon. Set aside.
2. Whip the egg whites until they peak. Add the remaining sugar and whip for another minute.
3. Fold one third of the egg whites into the yolk mixture. When mixed, very gently fold in the remaining whites.
4. Sift the flour and potato starch together. Carefully fold the flour mixture into the egg mixture. Do not overmix.
5. Pour the batter into a buttered, floured cake mold (9 inch). Bake in the oven at 325 degrees for about 15 to 20 minutes. (Test with a needle or fork; if the needle comes out clean, the cake is done.)

Biscuit à la Cuillère

Ladyfingers

Makes 24 to 30 ladyfingers

6 eggs, separated
¾ cup sugar
1 teaspoon vanilla or orange flower water
½ cup flour
powdered sugar (to dust tops)

1. Put the yolks and sugar into a warm bowl. Beat the mixture until it is creamy, fluffy, and almost white.
2. Add the vanilla or, better, orange flower water. Sift in the cake flour a third at a time, cutting and folding with a spatula.
3. Beat the egg whites until stiff. Fold them into the batter.
4. Cover a baking sheet with parchment paper. Put the mixture into a pastry bag with a medium-large, plain round tube. Force the batter onto the paper in fingers 3 inches long and 1 inch wide.
5. Lightly sprinkle with powdered sugar. Bake in a slow oven (275 to 300 degrees) until crisp and light brown.
6. Using a metal spatula, remove ladyfingers from the paper while warm. Cool on a rack.

Macarons

Macaroons

Makes 12 to 18 cookies

4¼ ounces almonds
8½ ounces sugar
1 to 2 egg whites
½ teaspoon vanilla
¼ teaspoon almond extract
powdered sugar (to dust macaroons)

1. Put the almonds in the bowl of a food processor. Run until the almonds are ground into a powder. Mix in the sugar, a small amount at a time. Remove from food processor and place in a bowl.
2. Stir half an egg white into the almond mixture. When mixed, add the other half of the white. Mix again. Keep on adding half an egg white until the almond mixture is completely absorbed and the batter is soft but not runny. Add vanilla and almond extract to taste.
3. Put the almond mixture in a pastry bag. Squeeze out macaroons the size of a dollar piece onto a baking sheet covered with parchment paper. Very lightly spray the macaroons with water. Sprinkle with powdered sugar and bake at 300 degrees for about 15 minutes.

Marquise au Chocolat

Serves 6

5 ounces semi-sweet chocolate
7 egg yolks
8½ ounces sugar
10½ ounces unsalted butter
5½ ounces cocoa powder
1 cup heavy cream
24 ladyfingers (see recipe page 208)
1 cup cold coffee (expresso)

1. Melt the chocolate in a double boiler or in a bain-marie. Let it melt slowly.
2. In a medium bowl put the egg yolks and sugar. Beat with a wire whip until fluffy.
Slowly incorporate the melted chocolate, lifting up the mixture with a wooden spatula, to
make it light and airy.
3. In another bowl, work the butter until soft and smooth. Add the cocoa powder to it, a
small amount at a time. Beat with a whip.
4. Incorporate the butter-cocoa paste into the egg yolk–sugar mixture. Mix well.
5. Whip the cream and add it to the chocolate mixture. Give it another quick whip. Place
in refrigerator.
6. Soak the ladyfingers in cold expresso coffee. Line the bottom and sides of an oblong,
3 inch high mold with the ladyfingers. Fill with the chocolate mixture. Refrigerate for
about 6 hours.
7. Serve with sauce au café (see page 222).

You can buy the ladyfingers, but making your own is a lot of fun and they will taste so
much better.

Mousse au Chocolat

Serves 4

3½ tablespoons unsalted butter
5 tablespoons sugar
7 ounces semi-sweet chocolate
6 eggs, separated
2 ounces dark rum (Barbencourt preferred)

1. Melt the butter and chocolate in a bain-marie until smooth. Add sugar. Mix with a spoon until everything is very smooth. Put aside and let cool.
2. When the mixture is cool, add the egg yolks one at a time. Keep on mixing until completely smooth. Add the rum.
3. Beat the egg whites until stiff. Add them, one spoonful at a time, to the chocolate mixture. Mix thoroughly.
4. Spoon the mixture into individual serving dishes. Refrigerate for about 4 hours.
5. Decorate the mousse with whipped cream laced with Barbencourt or another dark rum.

Mousse au Chocolat Blanc

White Chocolate Mousse

Serves 8

12 ounces white chocolate
6 ounces unsalted butter
5 eggs, separated
½ cup sugar

1. Place the white chocolate in a small pan. Let the chocolate melt over a bain-marie or over very low heat.
2. In another pan, melt the butter.
3. Put the melted white chocolate in a bowl. Slowly add the butter. Using a wire whip, beat both ingredients until well mixed. Add 5 egg yolks, one at a time. Keep on beating until the mixture is nice and smooth.
4. Beat the egg whites until they start to stiffen. Sprinkle in the sugar, a little bit at a time. Continue beating until the whites are firm.
5. Using a wooden spoon, fold ⅓ of the egg whites into the chocolate mixture. Blend well, then add the remaining egg whites.
6. Spoon the mousse into ramekins or coupes. Refrigerate overnight.
7. Serve the mousse with sauce au café on the side (see page 222).

If you are a white chocolate fan, this is it. You can't stop dipping your fingers into the mousse.

Mousse au Café

Coffee Mousse

Serves 8

8 egg yolks
5 ounces sugar
1 ounce coffee liqueur
1 ounce coffee extract
4¼ ounces unsalted butter, melted
3 cups heavy cream

1. Put the yolks, sugar, coffee extract, and coffee liqueur into a bowl. Whip over low heat or in a double boiler until it gets fluffy and light like a sabayon (about 12 minutes). Add the melted butter and keep whipping. Remove from the heat.
2. Whip the cream until it is firm. Incorporate the cream into the cooled coffee mousse. Mix well.
3. Spoon the mousse into small ramekins or a coupe. Refrigerate for 3 hours before serving.

Serve with a chocolate sauce:
Melt 9 ounces of semi-sweet chocolate in 1½ cups water over low heat. Add a little sugar to taste. Stir until the sugar dissolves. Bring sauce to a simmer and stir for 2 minutes. Remove from heat and let cool briefly. Add 1 ounce of Cognac. Strain sauce through a fine sieve. Cool before serving.

This is one of my favorite cold desserts. It is so light, so tasty. If you plan on keeping this mousse for a day or two, add 1 leaf or 1 teaspoon of gelatin to the mixture before you add the cream. Make sure you dissolve the gelatin first in cold water.

Velours Glacé aux Deux Chocolats

Chocolate Velvet

Serves 4

2 cups heavy cream
2 ounces white chocolate
3 egg yolks
⅓ cup sugar
1 teaspoon vanilla
2 tablespoons green Chartreuse
2 ounces bitter-sweet chocolate

1. In a heavy saucepan, combine the cream and the white chocolate (broken into small pieces). Bring slowly to a boil over low heat, stirring occasionally. This will take about 5 minutes. Remove from heat and whisk to dissolve the white chocolate totally.
2. Combine the egg yolk and sugar. Return the saucepan to the heat and gradually combine the egg and sugar mixture into the cream and chocolate mixture. Cook over medium heat, stirring occasionally, until the mixture is thick enough to coat a spoon. This will take about 7 minutes. The mixture should be glossy with no foam. Remove from heat and whisk to stop cooking.
3. Add the vanilla and green Chartreuse. Put mixture in an ice cream machine. Run machine until ice cream starts to thicken.
4. Meanwhile, finely grate the bitter-sweet chocolate. Add to the ice cream. Return to ice cream machine for a minute.

A wonderful ice cream, the French version of chocolate chip.

Soufflé aux Framboises

Raspberry Soufflé

Serves 6

12½ ounces fresh raspberries
5 ounces sugar
1 lemon
3 egg yolks
12 egg whites

1. In a mixer put the raspberries, 3 ounces of sugar, and the juice of ¼ lemon. Run until smooth. Add the egg yolks and run mixer again for a few seconds. Pour the mixture into a large bowl.
2. Using a brush, butter the inside of 6 soufflé bowls (4 inches wide). Sprinkle the inside with sugar. Get rid of the excess sugar by turning the bowls upside down.
3. Using a balloon whip, beat the egg whites with a pinch of salt until firm but not dry. Pour in the remaining 2 ounces of sugar, a small amount at a time. Keep on whipping until all of the sugar has been incorporated.
4. Take a quarter of the egg whites and incorporate it into the raspberry purée. Then fold in the remaining egg whites. (Use a wooden spoon for this procedure.)
5. Fill up the soufflé bowls with the batter. Bake at 325 degrees for about 12 to 16 minutes. Serve immediately with a raspberry coulis on the side (see page 223).

The lightest soufflé I have ever put together, this soufflé can be a little tricky. Make sure not to overcook it; it will fall right away, since there are no binding agents but egg yolks. Definitely a challenge.

Soufflé Orange

Orange Soufflé

Serves 4

2 oranges (for zest)
2¾ cups sugar
6 egg whites
1 cup crème pâtissière (see page 221)
1 ounce Grand Marnier
1 teaspoon orange flower water

1. Using a potato peeler, peel all of the skin off both oranges. Make sure you remove all of the white pith from the skin. Save the oranges for some other use.
2. Bring a quart of water to a boil; drop in the orange peel and blanch for 3 minutes. Repeat this procedure two more times, making sure to change the water each time. Drain the skins.
3. Put the sugar and 2 cups of water into a pot. Bring to a boil and add the orange peel. Lower the heat and cook slowly for 3 hours. Do not boil.
4. Remove the skins from the syrup and drain on a rack for 2 to 3 hours until dry. (These steps may be performed a day ahead).
5. Whip the egg whites until stiff.
6. Chop up the candied orange peel and add to the pâtissière. Pour in the Grand Marnier and the orange flower water. Return to heat, stirring until just warm.
7. When the pâtissière is warm, remove from heat and fold in the stiffly whipped egg whites.
8. Pour the mixture into a buttered, sugared soufflé mold. Bake for 20 minutes at 350 degrees. Serve immediately.

To save time, you can buy candied orange peel, all ready to use.

Soufflé au Chocolat (ou au Grand Marnier)

Chocolate (or Grand Marnier) Soufflé

Serves 4

6 egg whites
1 tablespoon sugar
1 cup crème pâtissière (see page 221)
2 tablespoons cocoa powder (or 2 ounces Grand Marnier)

1. Whip egg whites until stiff but not dry. Add sugar and whip for another minute.
2. Put crème pâtissière into a saucepan. Stir over medium heat until warm. Whip in cocoa powder (or Grand Marnier.) Remove pan from heat.
3. Gently fold in the egg whites.
4. Butter and sugar one large soufflé mold. Pour the mixture into the mold. Bake at 350 degrees for about 20 minutes, or until the soufflé has doubled in size and its top is lightly browned. The center of the soufflé should be very moist. Serve immediately.

Oeufs à la Neige

Floating Island

Serves 6

8 eggs, separated
21 ounces (2 cups, 5 ounces) granulated sugar
1 teaspoon vanilla
2 cups milk
1 pinch salt
1½ ounces peeled pistachio nuts

1. Whip together 8 egg yolks with 8½ ounces sugar for about 5 minutes. Add the vanilla. In a sauce pan, bring milk to a boil and remove from heat. Mix in egg yolk mixture and return to medium heat. Keep stirring with a wooden spoon until the custard starts to thicken. **Do not boil.** Remove from the heat and set the pot in a bowl of ice water to stop the custard from cooking.
2. Whip the egg whites to a firm peak. Add a pinch of salt and the remaining 12½ ounces of sugar. Continue whipping for a couple of minutes.
3. Butter and sugar an ovenproof bowl. Pour in the meringue. Place the bowl in a bain-marie and bake at 300 degrees for 30 to 40 minutes.
4. Let the meringue rest for a few minutes before unmolding it onto a platter. Pour the cold custard around the meringue and sprinkle with pistachios.

You can also serve the floating island with caramel custard (see page 220) and raspberry coulis (see page 223).

Floating Island on Nantucket – that makes sense. But apart from that, I love this dessert because my mother used to make it on Sundays when we were kids. It is very refreshing in the summer and so light we call it snow eggs in French.

Crème Anglaise

Custard Sauce

Serves 6

4¼ ounces sugar
4 egg yolks
1 cup milk
1 teaspoon pure vanilla extract

1. In a bowl, whip together the sugar and the yolks until they are light and fluffy.
2. In a saucepan, bring the milk to the boil. Remove pan from heat and incorporate hot milk into the sugar and egg mixture, whipping constantly. Add vanilla and whip again.
3. Pour mixture back into a saucepan. Stirring constantly with a wooden spoon, cook quickly for 2 to 3 minutes, or until the custard becomes the consistency of heavy cream.
4. Remove from heat and set pan in a bowl of ice water to stop the cooking process.

For some recipes you may wish to flavor the crème anglaise by mixing in one ounce of Calvados or another liqueur. Add the liqueur after the custard has finished cooking.

I don't even know why it is called crème anglaise. I doubt very much that it originated across the Channel, but wherever it comes from, crème anglaise is a wonderful custard or dessert sauce. It is so very versatile. Crème anglaise is the base of ice cream and of Bavarian cream. It is used with many cakes as a sauce. I can even eat crème anglaise by itself. It is also very good with poached fruits.

Crème Anglaise au Caramel

Caramel Sauce

Makes 1¾ cups

6 ounces sugar
4 egg yolks
1 cup milk
1 teaspoon vanilla

1. Place 2 ounces of sugar in a small pan. Cover with water and bring to a boil. Reduce heat and keep cooking until caramel becomes light brown. Remove from heat and let cool.
2. In a bowl, whip together the remaining 4 ounces of sugar and the yolks until they are light and fluffy.
3. Pour the milk over the cooled caramel. Put the pan back on the heat, stirring to make sure that the caramel at the bottom of the pan has melted completely. Bring to a boil, then remove pan from heat.
4. Whipping constantly, incorporate the hot milk and caramel mixture into the sugar and egg mixture. Add the vanilla and whip again.
5. Pour mixture into a saucepan and return to the heat. Stirring constantly with a wooden spoon, cook for 2 to 3 minutes (or until the custard becomes the consistency of heavy cream).
6. Remove pan from heat and set it in a bowl of ice water to stop the cooking process.

Crème Pâtissiére

Pastry Cream (Soufflé Base)

Makes about 1 cup

1 cup milk
2 eggs
3½ ounces sugar
1⅓ ounces flour

1. Put the milk into a pan and bring it to a boil.
2. In a bowl, whip the eggs and the sugar until the mixture becomes fluffy. Slowly add the flour and keep stirring.
3. Pour the boiling milk into the egg mixture. Mix well.
4. Put everything back in the pan. Stirring constantly, bring to a boil and cook for 2 to 3 minutes. Be careful not to let the crème stick to the bottom of the pan and brown.

This base can be used for any dessert soufflé. Just add flavoring to the pâtissière and reheat it slightly before using.

Meringue Italienne

Italian Meringue

Makes enough to cover one 10 inch pie

3 egg whites
8½ ounces sugar
3⅓ ounces water

1. Put the sugar and water into a saucepan. Bring to a boil. Keep on cooking at low heat until it reaches the boulé stage (the ball). This occurs at about 245 degrees. If you don't have a candy thermometer, drop a little of the syrup into water; it will form a small, sticky ball. Keep the syrup warm, but do not cook it anymore.
2. Whip the egg whites to a stiff peak. Add the syrup and keep on whipping until thoroughly incorporated.

When cooled, Italian meringue can be used for many desserts (cakes, sorbets, etc.) instead of whipped cream. This kind of meringue does not have to cook in the oven.

Crème au Beurre

Butter Cream Frosting

Makes about 2 cups

¾ cup sugar
8 egg yolks
12 ounces unsalted butter, softened
a few drops vanilla

1. Put the sugar into a small saucepan. Cover it with water and bring to a boil. Keep on cooking at low heat until it reaches the filet stage (the thread stage) at about 230 degrees Fahrenheit.
2. Put the egg yolks in a bowl and whip in the syrup, a small amount at a time.
3. Take the bowl with the yolk and syrup mixture and set it on ice. Stir the mixture until it cools and becomes thick.
4. Add this cooled mixture to the previously softened butter. Whip in the vanilla. Keep on beating for a few minutes until all the ingredients are blended well together.

This is a basic crème au beurre recipe. The crème can now be flavored with many different ingredients: cocoa powder, praline paste, coffee, liqueurs, etc.

Sauce au Café

Coffee Sauce

Serves 6

2 cups milk
5 ounces sugar
2 teaspoons ground expresso
6 egg yolks

1. Put the milk and half of the sugar into a pot. Bring to a boil. Add the expresso grinds. Cover the pot and let it brew for 15 minutes.
2. Put egg yolks and remaining sugar in a bowl. Whip until fluffy. Add the coffee infusion and put back in the pot. Cook like you would a custard for about 3 or 4 minutes. Put the pot in ice water right away to stop the cooking process.

Coulis de Framboises

Raspberry Sauce

10 ounces raspberries, fresh or frozen (you can also use strawberries, blackberries, etc.)
6½ ounces sugar
juice of 1 lemon

1. Pick through the berries and remove all stems and leaves.
2. Put fruit, sugar, and lemon juice in the blender. Run until smooth.
3. Put the sauce through a fine sieve to get rid of all the seeds. Refrigerate.

This coulis de framboises can be served with a multitude of desserts.

Pâte Brisée

Basic Pastry (for Tarts, Quiche, etc.)

Makes about 2 pounds or three 10 inch tarts

16½ ounces all-purpose, unbleached flour
10 ounces unsalted butter, softened
1 egg
2 teaspoons salt
1½ tablespoons sugar (for desserts only)
3 ounces cold water

1. Place the flour in a bowl. Put the egg in the center. Add the salt, sugar (if needed), softened butter, and 3 ounces of cold water. Start mixing. If the pastry looks too dry, add a little more cold water. Keep on mixing until all the flour has been absorbed.
2. Wrap the dough in plastic wrap; chill well in refrigerator before using.

You can also make the dough in a food processor.

Pâte Sucrée

Sweet Dough (for Pies, Cookies, etc.)

Makes one 9 inch pie crust

4¼ ounces flour
1 egg
2 ounces sugar
1 pinch salt
2 ounces butter, softened
1½ tablespoons cold water

1. Place the flour in a bowl. Put the egg in the center. Add the sugar, salt, softened butter, and 1½ tablespoons cold water. Start mixing. If the dough looks too dry, you may have to add a little more cold water. Keep on mixing until all the flour has been absorbed.
2. Wrap the dough in plastic wrap. Chill well in the refrigerator before using.
3. If you intend to use the pâte sucrée for a tart shell baked before filling, here is what to do. Roll out the dough to a shy ¼ inch thick. Place it in the pie pan and trim the excess dough. Prick the bottom a few times with a fork. Cover the bottom with pie weights (little metal beads). Bake at 325 degrees for 10 to 15 minutes. Be very careful not to burn the crust. When cool, remove the pie weights. This kind of shell is very brittle, so be careful when handling it. The shell will stay crisp for a couple of days and does not need to be refrigerated.

You can also make the dough in a food processor.

Index

A

B

C

G

H

I

K

L

M

N

O

P